UNTYING KNOTS

UNTYING KNOTS
Navigating the Legal Landscape of Divorce

ISBN (paperback): 978-1-964046-29-7
ISBN (hardback): 978-1-964046-41-9

**Expert
Press**
www.ExpertPress.net

The information provided in this book is for informational purposes only
and is not intended to be a source of advice with respect to the material
presented. The information and/or documents contained in this book do not
constitute legal advice and should never be used without first consulting with
a lawyer. The publisher and the author do not make any guarantee or other
promise as to any results that may be obtained from using the content of this
book. To the maximum extent permitted by law, the publisher and the author
disclaim any and all liability in the event any information, commentary,
analysis, opinions, advice, and/or recommendations contained in this book
prove to be inaccurate, incomplete, or unreliable or result in any losses.

Although the author and publisher have made every effort to ensure that the
information in this book was correct at press time, the author and publisher
do not assume and hereby disclaim any liability to any party for any loss,
damage, or disruption caused by errors or omissions, whether such errors
or omissions result from negligence, accident, or any other cause. Content
contained or made available through this book is not intended to and does
not constitute legal advice, and no attorney- client relationship is formed. The
publisher and the author are providing this book and its contents on an "as is"
basis. Your use of the information in this book is at your own risk.

Editing by Ty Hager
Copyediting by Hannah Skaggs
Proofreading by Heather Dubnick
Text design and composition by Emily Fritz
Cover design by Casey Fritz

UNTYING KNOTS

Navigating the Legal Landscape of Divorce

JEFF STERLING HUGHES, JD

*Dedicated to my amazing teammates
at Sterling Lawyers, who serve clients enduring
family legal crises.*

CONTENTS

INTRODUCTION

Believe it or not, I *really* wish you weren't reading this book. I wish that "Til death do us part" were more the norm than the exception, and that the tragedy of divorce was something you hardly ever heard about instead of a sad fact that permeates the very fabric of our society.

But if wishes were horses, beggars would ride.

Since you *are* reading this book, it's likely that either you or someone you love is contemplating or going through a divorce. I'm truly sorry for that, and I hope the knowledge I'm about to share—gleaned over more than twenty years as a divorce attorney—can help you understand what the road ahead may look like and offer some ways to make that road as smooth as possible.

Long before I was an attorney focusing on family law, I was a child of divorce. I witnessed firsthand the emotional and financial toll it took on my parents; I felt the anxiety and misplaced feelings of guilt so many children of divorce experience. I had no idea that I would one day help thousands of people navigate the trauma of divorce. I certainly never thought I'd be writing a book about it.

As you embark on your own divorce journey, this book will provide insights into the nuanced decision-making process leading up to divorce, explore alternatives and dispel common myths that may cloud the path ahead. We'll delve into the crucial task of selecting the right divorce attorney (and just *why* it's so crucial), and I'll make the case for "fixed-rate" firms and tell you why I think this business model—used exclusively by my own firm, Sterling Lawyers, since 2016—should be the industry standard. I'll address issues of child custody, financial support, and property division, and provide guidance on negotiation strategies. I'll also offer perspectives on rebuilding, healing, and crafting a new narrative for life after divorce. Along the way, I'll include QR codes for videos that provide even more detail about various topics.

The legal landscape of divorce is complex—statutes and guidelines can vary not just from state to state but from jurisdiction to jurisdiction. As such, it's important to remember that, while I'm a lawyer, I'm not *your* lawyer. The guidance I provide in the pages that follow is not meant to be specific legal advice but rather my perspectives and observations from spending over two decades "in the trenches" and overseeing thousands of cases in my law firm.

As I said, I wish you weren't reading this book, but you are. You've got a bumpy road ahead—armed with knowledge, understanding, and a compassionate guide, you can navigate it with resilience and purpose to avoid the pitfalls that can make a tragic situation even worse.

SECTION I
Pre-Divorce

INTRODUCTION VIDEO

Let's face it: Divorce is a *big* step. The decision to end a marriage can have profound and far-reaching ramifications, impacting the lives of not just you and your spouse but also your children and—to a lesser but still significant degree—your friends, co-workers or employees, and extended family. Divorce is an upheaval. Its emotional toll is undeniable and unavoidable, invoking feelings of anger and grief, leaving all involved anxious and uncertain about the future. Its financial toll can be substantial even in the best of circumstances, and downright catastrophic in the worst. Assets may need to be divided, spousal support (or alimony) and child support paid, and, yes, attorneys hired.

Divorce isn't something you should go into blindly or in the heat of passion; you need to think it through.

You need to be aware of just how *different* your life, your spouse's life, and your children's lives will be on the other side.

Over the next few chapters, I'll walk you through many of the factors you should consider before taking such a big step. We'll look at the aforementioned costs—both emotional and financial—and explore how you might avoid heading down what will almost undoubtedly be a long and rocky road. I'll also debunk some common myths about divorce.

If, sadly, you reach the conclusion that your marriage cannot be salvaged, I'll help you navigate the next steps to find the right divorce attorney for your situation.

CHAPTER 1
Before You Divorce

Just as every person is totally unique in their own way, so too is every marriage. And so too is every divorce. Long-term relationships are an intricate tapestry of shared experiences and mutual growth, delicately interwoven with the threads of love, passion, and commitment.

Sometimes the threads come unraveled. Sometimes they become frayed. And sometimes it seems that the damage is beyond repair—that issues stemming from a lack of communication, or infidelity, or finances, or substance abuse, or any of a myriad of conflicts have torn the fabric of the relationship to shreds.

Divorce may seem unavoidable.

But is it?

TRY EVERYTHING ELSE FIRST
TO SAVE YOUR MARRIAGE

Is Reconciliation Possible?

As I'm a divorce attorney, you may be surprised to learn that the first thing I recommend to potential clients is that they consider every avenue to reconciliation before they hire me. Why? Because I'm not in the business of breaking up salvageable marriages. And because once the initial steps have been taken, that bell can be hard to un-ring. Once your spouse *knows* you've taken those steps—once they know divorce is on the table—any chances of reconciliation may be destroyed.

Divorce creates its own inertia. Telling your spouse that you're considering it can create a heightened emotional atmosphere and feelings of anxiety. The mere mention of divorce may be perceived as a serious breach of the marital bond, leading to feelings of betrayal, sadness, and resentment. It can escalate tensions and hinder open communication, making it challenging for both partners to engage in constructive dialogue about their concerns and the underlying issues in the relationship. Problems that, in their mind, may have seemed solvable no longer *feel* solvable. The revelation that one spouse is contemplating divorce may also trigger defensive reactions, making it difficult for the couple to approach the situation with the empathy and understanding necessary for successful reconciliation efforts.

A lot of people come to me thinking they'll be happier if they divorce, not realizing they may just create a new set of problems. The process of divorce is hard; it's long, it's stressful, it's grinding. You may be relinquishing control of many areas of your life, your spouse's life, and your children's lives to a judge you've likely never met.

It may seem to you that the issues in your relationship are insurmountable, and any efforts to reconcile would be futile. But when you weigh those issues against the upheaval wrought by divorce, they may not be as insurmountable as you think.

Explore marriage counseling. There are many qualified and experienced counselors out there, and counseling comes in many different forms: from traditional face-to-face sessions to online platforms that offer flexibility in scheduling. If you belong to a church, you may be able to seek guidance from your pastor. Additionally, some counselors specialize in specific issues, such as communication problems, infidelity, or substance abuse, ensuring that the therapy is tailored to unique challenges within your marriage.

Another option might be "intensive marriage counseling." Often referred to as marriage or couples' "retreats," intensive counseling is a concentrated and immersive approach to addressing relationship issues. These programs typically span several days and provide couples with a focused environment to delve deep into their challenges and work toward resolution together. The extended duration allows for a more in-depth exploration of issues, offering couples the opportunity to engage in extensive communication exercises, therapeutic interventions, and skill-building activities. Intensive marriage counseling often takes place in serene and neutral settings, away from the distractions of daily life, facilitating a heightened focus on the relationship. The concentrated nature of these programs can be particularly beneficial for couples facing significant challenges, providing a dedicated space to rebuild trust, enhance communication, and strengthen the foundation of the marriage.

When my marriage was in trouble, an intensive retreat was the route my wife and I chose. And we benefited greatly from three diffcrent retreats over a few years.

Regardless of the route you choose, it's important to research and choose a counselor who aligns with your and your spouse's goals and values, creating a supportive environment to foster open communication so that you can work toward a healthier, more fulfilling relationship.

Don't take reconciliation off the table. It may seem a herculean and even financially costly effort, but—compared to the chaos, upheaval, and financial cost of a divorce—it may be worth it.

Other Divorce Alternatives

OTHER DIVORCE ALTERNATIVES

If reconciliation just doesn't seem possible, other options are still available before you take the life-changing step of ending your marriage.

Trial separation involves living apart for a specified period without legal formalities, allowing spouses to assess the impact of separation on their relationship. In my experience, it's almost always a prelude to a divorce, as it simply enables couples to drift further apart. For some, however, it can be a positive experience, especially if both spouses are committed to doing everything they can during the trial separation to stay married, such as working on themselves in individual counseling.

Legal separation, available in most states, involves a formal court process during which couples live separately but remain legally married. The legal process itself looks very similar to divorce; it addresses issues such as spousal support, child custody, and property division but without finalizing the divorce. If, after a specified period of time (typically one year), either spouse wants to make the dissolution of the marriage permanent, it's usually just a matter of filing a one-page document to convert the legal separation to a judgment of divorce.

Annulment is a legal declaration that a marriage is void, essentially stating that it never legally existed. Annulments are pretty rare, and the grounds on which a spouse can seek one—situations like fraud or misrepresentation, bigamy, lack of consent due to mental incapacity, underage marriage without proper consent, and marriage under duress or coercion—vary from state to state. A legal annulment is entirely different from a religious annulment.

Determining Your Divorce Goals

If exhaustive efforts at reconciliation haven't worked out, if trial separation has been tried and failed, and if annulment just isn't an alternative (as I mentioned, it's probably not), divorce may unfortunately be your last option.

Think it through. Think about it harder than you've ever thought about *anything*.

What will this divorce accomplish? How do you envision your life on the other side? Clients often answer these questions with some variation of "I just want to be happier" or "It's what's best for everybody."

That won't cut it. You have to dive *much* deeper. Ask yourself questions about living arrangements, financial stability, parenting considerations, social support, career and personal goals, and legal and practical matters. Let these questions serve as a guide—and even a warning—as you carefully assess your readiness for the emotional, financial, and practical changes divorce entails. By reflecting on these aspects of the decision, you can gain a clearer understanding of your expectations. That clarity will allow you to make informed decisions and develop strategies for coping with the challenges that may arise during and after the divorce process.

I believe this introspection is a contributing factor to about a third of my initial consultations *not* going through with it (I'm just estimating, but I don't think I'm far off). Once they grasp just how much of an ordeal it's going to be, and all the far-reaching ramifications they hadn't even considered, taking every possible step to *avoid* divorce seems less of an uphill battle.

And I'm fine with that—much prefer it actually.

Breaking the News

BREAKING THE NEWS TO YOUR SPOUSE

You've tried reconciliation, through long talks with your spouse or with marriage counselors or with a combination of both. You've tried separation. Nothing's worked.

You've thought about it, then thought about it, then thought about it some more. You've looked at your life under a microscope, then pictured how every aspect of it is going to change. If you have children, you've agonized over what this is going to mean for them.

Divorce is the sad but inescapable conclusion.

Now you need to have one of the most painful conversations of your life. Then, if you have kids, an even more painful conversation.

Telling Your Spouse

Regardless of any animosity you may be feeling toward them, or the animosity they feel toward *you*, it's important to remember that you once committed your life to your spouse, and they committed theirs to you. You were once going to live "happily ever after" together.

Keep in mind that you've been thinking about this for a while now. You've grappled with the emotions and had time to process them. This most likely won't be the case with your spouse.

Don't use your decision as a weapon. Don't drop a grenade. Don't play the blame game. As we discussed, this is going to be a long and trying road, and if you want the process to go more smoothly for everyone, you'll be sensitive and compassionate and empathetic to the shock and betrayal they may feel.

Choose a quiet and private location—no kids, no interruptions—for the initial conversation, but be aware that this will most likely just be the first of several. It may take as much time (or longer) for your spouse to process as it took for you to struggle with making the decision in the first place.

Do not tell your spouse that you're filing for divorce by serving them with the papers. Getting things started on such a contentious note never, *ever* works out well for any of those involved. A contentious divorce is longer, more painful, and more expensive (sometimes exponentially so) than one that—if not necessarily amicable—is at least devoid of fireworks.

BREAKING THE NEWS TO YOUR CHILDREN

Telling Your Children

As you might imagine (or perhaps know through first-hand experience), the true victims of divorce are always the kids. No matter how hard you think this might be on you, it's going to be harder on them. Even if there is abuse involved (in which case most child specialists agree that divorce is actually *better* for the well-being of the children), chances are you're about to upend the only life they've ever known. They'll never forget this moment.

Your divorce can instill feelings of doubt and betrayal that may haunt them for the rest of their lives. Often children hold themselves personally responsible.

Don't leave it to your spouse to tell them. No matter the acrimony that exists between the two of you, presenting this to your children as a united front with your spouse is crucial. Don't let it be an impromptu discussion in which they are unsuspecting that heavy news is about to be delivered. This should be a planned discussion, at a time when the children do not have to be anywhere else immediately afterwards; they will need privacy and time to process. Be prepared to have honest, open conversations (as with your spouse, this shouldn't be a "one and done") about your decision. Be honest, but do not overshare. Do not discuss who chose to proceed with the divorce or the details as to why a divorce is necessary. Do not make promises about what will or will not change (i.e. school district, remaining in the home, what holidays will look like, etc.) unless you are absolutely certain of those issues. Reassure them they are the priority, that this isn't their fault and your love for them is unwavering. With younger kids especially, if possible, you should try to have a series of conversations before you and your spouse actually separate. It's going to take them some time to process, and they'll have questions, then more questions. Be patient and help them get used to the idea.

Don't tell your children you're divorcing until you've made a definite decision. Don't dangle the prospect over their heads as you and your spouse go through a series of separations and reunifications that only serve to prolong their doubts and fears.

Divorce is never a win-win situation. In fact, to a certain degree, it's much more likely to be lose-lose. Before you commit to ending your marriage, you should do everything under the sun to avoid it. And once you've made the decision, it's crucial that you do everything possible to ensure it's not more painful—especially to your beloved children—than it has to be.

CHAPTER 2
Common Divorce Myths

Many people—especially those who haven't gone through it before—go into divorce with unrealistic expectations. For most of their lives up to this point, they hadn't even *thought* about divorce except as something that happened to somebody else. Most of what they know therefore comes anecdotally, through friends or family members or through subplots in books, TV shows, or movies.

They create in their mind a picture of how their own divorce will go based on this limited knowledge, as well as on their own emotions and biases toward the spouse they're divorcing.

Chances are this picture is based on myths.

There's an old quote, often attributed to Mark Twain, that goes, "It ain't what you don't know that gets you into trouble. It's what you know for sure that just ain't so."

In this chapter, I hope to bring your expectations down to earth by debunking some common myths and unrealistic expectations that you may "know for sure" but that "just ain't so."

Most of these will also be covered in more detail later in the book.

Divorce Myth 1: "My divorce case can be won."

MYTH 1: YOU WIN YOUR DIVORCE

No. Your case can't be won.

Why? Because, as I've mentioned, there are no winners in divorce.

As a lawyer, I'm often asked, "What's your winning percentage?" That's an easy one: It's zero. It's not about winning. It's about mitigating the loss. It's about having a bumpy landing instead of a fiery crash.

A lot of people see divorce as a battle and approach it with that mindset, thinking they should go on the offensive and attack the other side. That's an emotional and dangerous perspective that will only inspire the other side to retaliate and attack you. Throwing stones not only prolongs the pain, but it distracts from the important issues that need to be addressed. Most states provide for "no fault" grounds for divorce; this is because the court wants to minimize this exact behavior. Taking an aggressive, litigious posture is unlikely to render better results for you. And it's going to greatly increase the cost.

That's not to say there aren't victories to be won. There will be skirmishes over issues like property division or child custody and support that—with the right attorney and smart strategies—can result in a favorable outcome. But those strategies typically include high-level communication, information sharing and skilled negotiation—not mudslinging. Taking a high-conflict approach won't make you a winner.

At the end of it all, though, you're still going to be divorced. And if you have minor children, you'll have ruined any chance you had of a healthy co-parenting relationship with your ex.

MYTH 2: I DO ALL THE WORK IN THE RELATIONSHIP, SO I SHOULD GET MOST OF THE ASSETS

Divorce Myth 2: "I do all the work in the relationship, so I should get most of the assets."
Au contraire. (That will be my sole excursion into French; I'm more of a Latin guy.)

Most often, this misconception is held by the main breadwinner in a marriage. They feel like, "I earned all the money, I should keep most of the stuff we bought with that money."

This "just ain't so" for a couple of reasons: First, the division of assets in a divorce is not based solely on individual contributions during the marriage. Courts typically aim for equitable distribution, considering various factors such as the duration of the marriage, financial contributions, and nonfinancial contributions like homemaking and childcare.

Second, relationships involve a complex interplay of responsibilities, and valuing one partner's contributions over the other's in a quantitative manner can oversimplify the dynamics. Courts recognize the multifaceted nature of contributions to a marriage, and attempting to quantify these merely in terms of workload or monetary earnings may not align with legal principles of fairness. Divorce settlements are designed to consider the overall well-being of both parties, taking into account the diverse aspects of their contributions throughout the marriage.

Similarly, a variation of this myth applies to child custody. One spouse will say, "I was the one who stayed home with the children, so I should get full custody."

Family courts prioritize the best interests of the child when determining custody arrangements. While being the primary caregiver may indeed be a factor, it's not going to be the sole determinant of custody. Courts assess various aspects of this issue, including the ability of each parent to provide a stable and supportive environment, the child's relationship with each parent, and the willingness of both parents to facilitate a healthy co-parenting relationship.

This myth also overlooks the importance of shared parental responsibilities and the evolving roles within modern families. Courts increasingly recognize the value of both parents in a child's life, and the emphasis is on fostering a meaningful relationship with both—even if the living arrangements are not equal. The focus is on creating a custody arrangement that supports the child's emotional and developmental needs rather than solely rewarding one parent based on historical caregiving roles.

MYTH 3: I'LL DO BETTER TAKING A CHANCE WITH THE JUDGE THAN NEGOTIATING WITH MY EX

Divorce Myth 3: "I'll do better taking a chance with the judge than negotiating with my ex."
This is hardly ever the case.

One of the key strategies in a divorce case is to maintain as much control as possible, or to at least minimize the number of issues *outside* your control. The judge will always be outside your control. Even if you and your spouse agree on everything, the judge will still have to sign off on that agreement.

Judges are human. Some days they wake up on the wrong side of the bed. They may have heartburn. Maybe they just had a fight with their spouse. Maybe you remind them of their spouse. There are a lot of ways things can go wrong.

By forgoing any negotiation with your spouse, you're expanding the element of your case over which you have the least control. You're increasing the odds you'll catch the judge on a bad day.

And courts are notoriously slow. If you want to guarantee that your divorce case will drag out for a couple of years (and thus be way more expensive), give it directly to the judge.

Also consider that your divorce agreement will affect virtually every aspect of your life for years to come. Do you really want one person, whom you barely even know, to decide all the particulars? The judge will base decisions on an extremely limited set of data points over just a short amount of time, stretched in small increments over a period of months (or longer). Negotiation—through any of the means we'll cover later—is by far, both financially and timewise, the most efficient way to go.

MYTH 4: THE JUDGE WILL
PUNISH MY EX

Divorce Myth 4: "The judge will punish my ex."
That's really not how it works.

I hear this one a lot, usually from a spouse who's seeking a divorce due to some sort of egregious behavior (like adultery, physical abuse, or substance abuse) by the other spouse. And it's totally understandable; after all, you've been *hurt* by your ex. You're justifiably angry. You don't just want a divorce, you want *justice*. Isn't that what the legal system's for?

Well . . . yes and no. It basically comes down to how you define justice.

Your judge may very well agree that your spouse's deeds are reprehensible. But divorce law doesn't give judges a lot of leeway to actually punish those types of behavior. Sure, your spouse's transgressions will certainly be considered in certain aspects of your case—particularly those that might impact the well-being of any children— but if you're expecting the judge to exact retribution on your behalf, you're going to be disappointed.

Disenchanting yourself from the notion of revenge is also an important part of acclimating yourself to the idea of reasonable negotiation with your spouse, which—as I've said before and I'll say again—can be crucial to making your divorce as smooth and painless as possible.

 MYTH 5: I'LL GET A BETTER RESULT WITH A MALE OR FEMALE ATTORNEY OR JUDGE

Divorce Myth 5: "I'll get a better result with a male (or female) attorney or judge."

In my experience, through the thousands of divorce cases I and my firm have seen, this "just ain't so."

Are there exceptions? Sure. But for every judge or attorney who adheres to common gender stereotypes, there's a long list of those who don't. You may have this idea that male judges or attorneys are more assertive or aggressive, and female judges or attorneys are more empathetic and compassionate. You may think you want a judge or attorney of your own gender because "they'll get it." Or you may think having an attorney of the opposite gender will demonstrate to the judge that you can't be as bad as your spouse says you are.

Pointless. There are so many things you're going to have to think long and hard about throughout your divorce. The gender of your judge or attorney isn't one of them.

MYTH 6: I DESERVE FIFTY-FIFTY TIME
WITH MY CHILDREN

Divorce Myth 6: "I deserve fifty-fifty time with my children."

In a perfect world, this might be the case. But it's not a perfect world.

Child custody arrangements can be immensely complex, considering factors such as stability, emotional well-being, and the ability of each parent to provide a supportive environment for the children. Courts also weigh factors such as work schedules, geographical distances, and the child's age or preferences.

It's all about what's best for *them*. So, yes, you may get equal custody. But it's speculative.

This would also be a good time to get in the habit of eliminating the word *my* when referring to your children. In my experience, judges have a real distaste for such overtly proprietary language. Get used to saying "*our* kids."

You're not the only parent. In my experience, judges don't like to hear otherwise.

 MYTH 7: MY LAWYER MUST DESPISE MY
EX AS MUCH AS I DO AND PROVE IT

Divorce Myth 7: "My lawyer must despise my ex as much as I do and prove it."

This is an extremely common misconception, but that doesn't make it right.

It's just human nature sometimes: Your spouse has wronged you in a way that leaves you far beyond merely angry; you hate them with the white-hot fire of a thousand suns. They represent pure evil. And, by extension, so does the attorney representing them. Your lawyer is your ally in the battle between good and evil, and you don't want to see them all "buddy-buddy" with the other side. You don't want to see them invalidate your own hatred.

While, due to this common misperception, our firm has kind of an unwritten rule against getting too chummy with the opposing parties, we also make our clients aware that all-out warfare is massively counterproductive. It's going to drive up costs, it's going to prolong your case, and it's only going to heighten the stress and anxiety of an already stressful and anxiety-ridden process.

As your parents or grandparents may have told you, you don't want to cut off your nose to spite your face. A collaborative effort between your attorney and the other side will make things go much more smoothly. You'll also get a much better outcome.

MYTH 8: THIS DIVORCE IS ABOUT PRINCIPLE; I DESERVE WHAT'S FAIR

Divorce Myth 8: "This divorce is about principle. I deserve what's fair."

No, it's really not, and no, it's probably not going to seem entirely fair.

Standing on principle, using your divorce proceedings as an opportunity to get on a soapbox and condemn all the moral injustices inflicted by your spouse, may *feel* good. But it's not going to do anything to make your divorce go more smoothly or be less costly. Quite the opposite.

And sure, everybody deserves fairness, but what's "fair" is entirely a matter of perspective. What seems fair to you is usually be the polar opposite of what seems fair to your spouse. And neither of your perspectives will be the same as that of the judge, whose job it is to ensure that fairness is applied solely within the constraints of what's legal.

Usually, the best outcomes in a divorce fall somewhere in the middle. Accept that it's probably not going to seem entirely fair and will likely seem like less than you deserve.

MYTH 9: I CAN PROTECT MY ASSETS IN A DIVORCE

Divorce Myth 9: "I can protect my assets in a divorce."

Sorry. Most likely you can't, at least not entirely.

I have clients say to me, "We kept our assets and debts separate while we were married. Surely we can keep them separate now." If you go into a divorce thinking this is the case—and you don't have a prenuptial agreement that specifically spells it out—you're probably going to be disappointed.

If your state follows an "equitable distribution" protocol, your assets will be divided based on factors such the length of the marriage, each spouse's contributions, financial circumstances, and future needs. If your state is one of the handful that follows a "community property" protocol, all of your assets are basically put into one pile and split down the middle.

Yes, there are legal ways to protect *some* assets. The key here is "legal." Trying to skirt the law to hide assets from your spouse can seem tempting, but it will usually get you into hot water.

It's important to go into a divorce with your eyes wide open. Knowing the realities—differentiating between what you know for sure and what you know for sure that just ain't so—will help you to be better prepared for what's to come.

CHAPTER 3
Navigating the Maze— Choosing the Right Divorce Lawyer

The roller coaster ride that is divorce isn't a fun ride. Nobody buys a ticket or gets in line, eagerly awaiting the thrills. Passengers tend to be people who never wanted to ride it in the first place. Choosing the right lawyer to accompany you on this ride is a crucial step that can significantly impact every aspect of your divorce, from property division to child custody. The right lawyer can even help turn the roller coaster into a merry-go-round (albeit a decidedly less merry one).

In this chapter, we'll take a closer look at what you need to know to navigate the maze of "attorney shopping," beginning with the most obvious question: Do you even need an attorney? From there, we'll cover what to look for in an attorney, what to avoid, red flags during your initial consult, and questions to ask to make sure you're getting exactly the right lawyer for your unique situation.

DO YOU NEED A LAWYER?

Do You Need a Lawyer?

The short answer to this question is exactly the answer you would expect from a divorce attorney: a resounding "Yes."

The reason I give this answer probably isn't what you would expect, though. As I've told you, my firm and I try to talk clients *out* of hiring us. We're painfully and thoroughly aware of the damage a divorce can do, of the suffering it leaves in its wake. If you want to at least mitigate the anguish of what will inevitably be a sad and bumpy ride, you need a guide.

If, on the other hand, you want to prolong the nightmare, to turn bumps in the road into mountains and dips into perilous freefalls, by all means, DIY! You may think you're saving money, but in the vast majority of cases—particularly those involving multiple assets, debts, or acrimonious disputes over child custody or support— you'll find out the hard way that you're not.

Virtually the only exception to this rule is the rarest of divorce cases in which neither spouse has any real assets or debts, nor does the couple have children together.

Even in these cases, you should—at the very least—have a qualified attorney look over your divorce documents before you sign them.

I emphasize that because it's just that important. I've seen scores and scores of "simple" cases come back before a judge because something was missed on the front end.

Over the last decade or so, as people have become more and more confident about using internet sources to do their own research, they're hiring lawyers less often. Honestly, I think that's a net positive. But with something as uniquely complex as a divorce (especially if you have kids), it's far too risky—and the potential damage from missteps is far too costly and long-lasting—to go it on your own.

HOW TO FIND AND PICK YOUR LAWYER

Finding a Lawyer: What to Look for and What to Avoid

Finding the right divorce lawyer is a key step, and it's crucial to have someone in your corner who really understands the ins and outs of family law. Here are some traits to look for when searching for the perfect divorce lawyer and some red flags that will tell you to keep looking.

Experience and Expertise

You want a lawyer who's been around the block in family law, someone who really knows the ropes when it comes to divorce cases. Don't ask for advice from your friend the real estate attorney, and don't go to your cousin who just passed the bar. Make sure your prospective counsel has at least five years' experience specifically in family law, preferably with a focus on divorce, or works very closely with a team of other lawyers who have long experience in divorce.

The reasons for this are twofold: First, family law isn't like any other specialty. Divorce laws change all the time and vary by state. Some elements—such as local court procedures and specific filing requirements—even vary within specific counties.

Second (and I can't stress this enough), an experienced family law attorney in your area is going to know the judges. This isn't to say that there's necessarily a "good ole boy network," or that the assigned judge will give any sort of preferential treatment to your attorney; it just means your prospective lawyer will be familiar with nuances and tendencies of the local judges regarding various aspects of your case. Candidly, it's more important for your attorney to know the judge than to know the law.

Reputation

Ask around! Check online reviews and chat with friends or family who have gone through a divorce. When doing your internet research, pay attention not just to the overall rating but to how many reviews make up that rating. You want a lawyer with a lot of positive reviews. And don't just look at the overall ratings; read as many of the reviews as you can. Look for comments regarding the "soft skills" of your prospective lawyer, things like empathy, caring, and listening.

Also be aware that many "badges," such as "Rising Star" or "Best Lawyer," aren't necessarily as valid as they seem. Sure, some may be, but often these are either popularity contests or honors that can be bought. The number of detailed, positive reviews is a much better indicator of quality.

But don't stop at reviews. Dig deeper. Try to determine whether this attorney or their firm has had any disciplinary actions filed against them. In particular, look for complaints concerning any lack of communication with their clients. Both should be big red flags.

Communication Skills and Compatibility

In any divorce case, communication is key! Your lawyer should be someone who explains things to you in plain English and promptly returns your calls or emails. You're going to be working with this person a lot over the next months (or even years), and you'll share details of your life that you may feel uneasy sharing. Make sure you feel comfortable enough to be totally honest with them. Make sure you feel that this person who'll be representing you and negotiating on your behalf is exactly the right person to do so. Trust your gut during your first face-to-face meeting. You'll know.

Another element that falls into this category is your prospective lawyer's personality. You need a peacemaker, not a brawler. For example, be wary of attorneys who disparage your spouse or your spouse's counsel. As I talked about earlier, you may want them to hate the opposing party as much as you do, but this kind of adversarial approach is a certain route to a longer, more painful, and more costly divorce. Now, there's always the chance that your prospective lawyer is expressing animus toward your ex or their attorney because they think that's what you want them to do, and they're just trying to get your business. Either way, don't fall for it.

You should also avoid lawyers who name-drop, boast about previous clients, or promise you the moon and tell you they're going to take your ex "to the cleaners" or some such nonsense. That's just trash talk and not the mark of experienced and effective representation.

Cost and Fee Structure
Be upfront about fees, ask about any extra costs, and get a clear picture of what you're looking at financially. We'll take a deep dive into this in the next chapter.

Alternative Dispute Resolution Skills

Look for a lawyer who'll talk you through *all* of your options, including negotiation and mediation. Sadly, far too many attorneys look at cases solely through a cash-colored lens and are motivated to take the path of most resistance if it means more money for them.

If you sense this is the type of lawyer you're talking to, run!

QUESTIONS TO ASK YOUR PROSPECTIVE ATTORNEY

Questions for Your Prospective Attorney

After you narrow down your list of prospects and schedule an initial consultation (often free) with the attorney you think might be a good fit, you should arrive at the meeting armed with a specific list of questions. We covered many of these broadly above; some of the answers you may have discovered through research. It still doesn't hurt to get them from the horse's mouth, so to speak. Just earmark this page of the book and take it to the consult with you.

1. Experience and Specialization

- How long have you been practicing family law?
- Do you specialize in divorce cases, and what percentage of your practice is devoted to family law?

2. Approach and Strategy

- What approach do you typically take in divorce cases? (litigation, mediation, collaborative law, etc.)
- How do you see my case unfolding, and what strategy would you recommend?

3. Communication

- How do you prefer to communicate with clients? (email, phone, in-person meetings)
- Exactly who will I be dealing with at the firm? Who can I contact if I can't reach you?
- How often can I expect updates on my case?

4. Fees and Billing

- What is your fee structure? (hourly, flat fee, retainer)
- Will I be billed monthly or at least consistently?
- Are there additional costs I should be aware of, such as court fees or administrative expenses?

5. Realistic Expectations

- Based on the information I've provided, what are the likely outcomes of my case?
- What challenges or obstacles do you foresee, and how do you plan to address them?

6. Alternative Dispute Resolution

- Are you open to alternative dispute resolution methods, like mediation or collaborative divorce?
- In your experience, when is it beneficial to pursue these alternative methods?

7. Timeline

- How long do you anticipate it will take to resolve my case?
- What factors could delay the process?

8. Local Knowledge

- Are you familiar with the family court judges and procedures in this jurisdiction?
- Have you handled cases in this specific county before?

9. Client References

- Can you provide references from previous clients who had similar cases?
- What do past clients say about working with you?

10. Potential Outcomes

- What are the potential outcomes of my case in terms of property division, alimony, child custody, and support?
- How will you work to achieve the best possible outcome for me?

11. Availability

- How accessible are you if I have questions or concerns?
- Do you have a team or support staff, and how can I reach them if needed?

Again, you may already have the answers to some of these questions; you may also have other questions. Ask them all.

Toward the end of the meeting, it's always a good idea to ask your prospective lawyer to "play back" the highlights of your talk—to summarize your case and their strategy based on your unique situation.

Finding the right divorce lawyer is like picking a trusted ally to navigate uncharted waters with you. This person will be your legal confidant, helping you untangle the complexities of divorce while offering much-needed support during a challenging time. The right lawyer not only brings legal expertise to the table but also understands the emotional intricacies involved. It's about finding someone who listens, communicates clearly, and advocates fiercely for your best interests. In essence, your divorce lawyer becomes your partner in crafting a new chapter of your life, and the right choice can make all the difference in your ability to achieve a fair and satisfactory resolution for your unique situation.

CHAPTER 4
More than Money—the True Costs of Divorce

THE TRUE COSTS OF DIVORCE

The true costs of divorce are far from just financial. They extend into the realm of profound emotional tolls, echoing the stages of grief first articulated in the bestselling book *On Death and Dying*.[1] Much like those coping with the loss of a loved one, those navigating divorce often find themselves cycling through denial, anger, bargaining, depression, and acceptance.

---

1   Elisabeth Kübler-Ross, *On Death and Dying* (University of Chicago Press, 1969).

The Death of a Marriage

1. Denial

At the outset of divorce, denial can be a potent defense mechanism. Your mind refuses to grasp the reality of the situation. Instead it clings to persistent false hopes that the marriage might somehow be salvaged and that the emotional pain can be stifled by believing that things will magically return to the way they once were.

2. Anger

As the realization of the irreversible nature of divorce sets in, anger rears its ugly head. Resentment, frustration, and a sense of betrayal overwhelm you, directed toward your ex-spouse, yourself, or even the circumstances that led you here. It's a tumultuous period of navigating through intense emotions and grappling with the profound changes divorce brings.

3. Bargaining

In the bargaining stage, you may find yourself desperately trying to reverse the situation. Bargaining often involves reflecting on what could have been done differently, imagining scenarios in which reconciliation is possible, and even striking internal deals to turn back time. It's a vulnerable phase marked by a yearning for what has been lost.

4. Depression

The weight of the divorce settles heavily during the depression stage. Feelings of sadness, loneliness, and despair replace the anger (though sometimes not completely). The enormity of the changes—to your own life, to your children's lives—becomes palpable, and you may grapple with a profound sense of loss, mourning not just the end of the relationship but also the dreams and aspirations tied to it.

5. Acceptance

In time, with introspection and healing, you'll gradually move toward acceptance. This doesn't necessarily mean joy or happiness; rather, it signifies an understanding of the new reality. Acceptance is a crucial stage for you to begin to rebuild your life, acknowledging the pain of the past but also embracing the potential for a different and fulfilling future.

Of course, everybody's different; every divorce is totally unique from every other divorce. Not everyone will go through all of these stages—but most will go through at least some version of most of them. I've seen people who seem to have it all together fall apart and become shells of their former selves for long periods of time (in some cases, even years). And I've seen people who didn't seem to have it all together handle their divorces much better than I had expected.

Adding to the emotional vulnerability that divorce brings, it can also be just downright stressful. According to the Holmes-Rahe Stress Scale, divorce is ranked the second-highest stressor for humans, second only to the death of a spouse.[2] It is, after all, the death of a marriage. And the longer the process goes on, the more stressful it becomes—an excellent reason to (a) find the right lawyer, and (b) not approach your divorce as an acrimonious battle.

But you don't have to just ride it out. There's help out there. Professional counseling can be a valuable option, with a licensed therapist providing a confidential space for you to navigate your emotions and develop coping mechanisms. "Divorce coaching" is an emerging resource offering personalized guidance and strategies to navigate the complexities of separation. (Be sure to do your research, though; divorce coaches aren't required to undergo any special training, and they can often get their licenses or certificates online.) Support groups, whether in person or online, can provide a communal space to share experiences and receive empathetic advice. Friends and family can form a crucial support network, offering trust and love during this challenging time.

2   Kellie Marksberry, "The Holmes- Rahe Stress Inventory," American Institute of Stress, February 11, 2022, https://www.stress.org/holmes-rahe-stress-inventory.

Many people feel uncomfortable about divulging their innermost thoughts to a stranger (or group of strangers). They're just not comfortable with sharing—that's not the type of person they are. Others may fear that what they tell their therapist may somehow end up in court. And yet others think their ex may use the fact that they're getting therapy as a sign they're unfit to have child custody.

Regarding the first of these, all I can tell you is that you would be amazed at how much better an objective, experienced perspective can make you feel. I highly recommend overcoming that particular reticence. As far as the fear that your therapist's records could be subpoenaed and your deepest, darkest secrets revealed in open court, therapists are bound by professional and ethical standards—just like attorneys—to maintain the privacy of their clients. In most jurisdictions, therapists can't be compelled to disclose information shared during therapy unless there's an imminent risk of harm to the client or others. That being said, the legal landscape can vary, and it's important to be aware of the specific laws in your area.

When it comes to your ex using your therapy as a weapon to sully you in the eyes of the judge, my experience has been that the inverse is more often true: It takes a bigger person to admit they need help and to actually seek it out than it does to defiantly resist the notion of oneself as flawed. It takes humility. It takes a willingness to go above and beyond. Judges usually like that.

The Financial Costs

None of the above is meant to diminish the very real fact that a divorce can also be financially draining. How much so will be determined to a significant degree by your choice of lawyer. Whether your attorney charges hourly (the traditional method) or offers fixed-rate legal services can play a huge role in the equation.

Fixed-Rate Billing Advantages

As I covered briefly in the introduction of this book, my firm transitioned to exclusively fixed-rate billing in 2016. Now, when I say, "fixed rate," I'm not talking about those cut-rate "bargain" divorces you find online for five hundred bucks. You get what you pay for, so that amount will usually just get you someone to file your paperwork. You probably won't get real representation. You probably won't get someone who'll negotiate on your behalf or—in many cases—even meet with you.

I'm talking about getting the same professional level of representation that you would if you were paying an hourly fee. That's what my firm does. Although these types of firms are by no means common, they're more common now than they used to be. If you can find one in your area—and if they check off all the boxes we discussed in the last chapter—I'd highly recommend going that route. Here are just a few of the reasons.

- **Predictability.** When contemplating the complexities of divorce proceedings, the prospect of financial uncertainty can be a daunting factor. Enter the fixed-rate divorce attorney—a beacon of predictability in a sea of uncertainty, affording you the luxury of clarity about precisely what financial commitment lies ahead.

- **Time.** The fixed-rate approach eliminates the anxiety associated with each invaluable passing minute during attorney-client interactions. You're not getting billed for every phone call, text, or email (those charges can quickly add up), so you don't feel pressured to keep communication with your lawyer—the bedrock of a smooth resolution—to an absolute minimum.

- **Stress reduction.** Unlike their hourly counterparts, who may inadvertently imbue every interaction with a sense of urgency tied to financial considerations, fixed-rate attorneys provide a more tranquil experience. This, in turn, fosters a collaborative and constructive environment for navigating the intricacies of divorce.

- **Efficiency.** The incentive to resolve cases quickly, as opposed to dragging them out longer for more money, underscores the commitment of fixed-rate attorneys to streamline the process. This efficiency translates into a more seamless and expedited progression through the various stages of divorce proceedings.

In essence, a fixed-rate divorce attorney is a strategic choice for those seeking financial transparency, reduced stress, and operational efficiency during a challenging life transition. For so many of the thousands of clients we've helped through this difficult time, fixed-rate billing has been a way to make a painful situation at least a little less painful.

CASH BURN DURING A DIVORCE

Cash Burn

Of course, the financial pain of divorce isn't limited to what your attorney charges. These are what I call the "cash burn" costs—because it can definitely seem like you're burning through your money. Most of these will be covered in more depth later in the book.

1. Splitting assets: The financial shuffle

So, you've got the house, the car, the shared account, and probably a few debts. Dividing all these things can be like solving a puzzle. You might need appraisers; you may have real estate fees to pay. And, of course, there could be tax implications.

2. Alimony and support: Continuous cash flow

Then there's alimony and/or spousal support. Figuring out who pays what and for how long is part of what you pay your lawyer to do, but the costs themselves, obviously, are up to you.

3. Kid-related costs: Supporting the young ones

If there are kids in the picture, child support is on the horizon. It's not just for the basics, like food and shelter. It's for school costs, doctor visits, and extracurricular activities. You want what's best for your kids; the court's job is to ensure they get it. I promise you they'll take it very seriously.

4. Double living costs: Managing two households

Divorce often means setting up separate households. Rent, mortgage, utilities—suddenly, you're juggling double the living costs. If you have children, it could mean buying new bedroom furnishings and toys, bicycles, etc.

5. Emotional well-being: Factoring in therapy costs

As we've discussed, the emotional toll of a split can lead to counseling or therapy. It's vital for your mental health (and, as I mentioned earlier, can be conducive to a better outcome in court), but it also comes with a cost. Investing in your well-being can be pricey but is undoubtedly necessary.

6. Tax considerations: Navigating IRS matters
The taxman doesn't take a break, not even
during a breakup. In addition to the possible tax
ramifications of the "asset shuffle," there are going
to be changes in filing status and in who claims
what deductions. Your divorce lawyer won't (and
shouldn't) also be a tax attorney.

7. Legal add-ons: More than just attorney fees
Apart from lawyer fees, there are other legal costs.
Filing fees, paperwork prep, and other court
mandates may fall outside the scope of the hourly
or fixed rate you're paying for representation, and
they can add up.

CAREER COSTS OF DIVORCE

Career Costs of Divorce
If you're going through—or at least contemplating—a
divorce, you're probably all too aware of the emotional
toll. You're living it. Depending on how far along you
are in the process, you're probably also getting a grasp on
the financial costs. But another cost of divorce is often
overlooked—you may or may not have seen already that
divorce can adversely affect your career.

Divorce can undoubtedly have a ripple effect that extends into your professional life. The emotional toll, legal commitments, and overall upheaval can create challenges that may negatively impact your career trajectory.

First, the emotional weight of a divorce can be all-consuming. Navigating the emotional roller coaster, from the decision to part ways to the actual separation, can easily distract you. The mental bandwidth required to handle personal matters might take away from your focus at work, leading to decreased productivity and lapses in concentration.

Moreover, the administrative demands of divorce, such as legal consultations, negotiations, court appearances, and paperwork, can necessitate time away from work. Balancing these commitments with professional responsibilities may result in increased absenteeism, affecting your attendance record and straining relationships with colleagues who may need to cover for your absences.

The stress associated with divorce can also impact your work. Emotional strain may manifest physically, leading to health issues that further contribute to absenteeism or decreased performance. The toll on your mental health can make it challenging to maintain your usual level of enthusiasm and engagement in your professional pursuits.

Ultimately, while divorce is a deeply personal matter, its impact often transcends the boundaries of personal life, seeping into the professional realm. Striking a balance between the demands of divorce and a steady professional trajectory requires resilience, effective time management, and a supportive work environment.

No matter what ads to the contrary you may see on TV or the internet, there is no such thing as a "cheap divorce." At its best, it's going to be painful; at its worst—and without a good lawyer and the emotional support of friends, family, and even counselors—it can be downright catastrophic.

SECTION II
The Divorce

As we've seen, embarking on the journey of divorce can be an emotionally charged and complex process, requiring careful navigation through legal intricacies. As a seasoned divorce attorney, I understand the myriad challenges individuals face when contemplating or undergoing the dissolution of a marriage. In this section of the book, we will delve into crucial aspects of the divorce process, and I'll offer practical insights and guidance to empower you through each stage.

We'll lay the foundation for a successful legal partnership, emphasizing effective communication and collaboration with your legal representative. Navigating the complexities of divorce requires a comprehensive understanding of various facets (many of which we've already touched on briefly), and we'll dive deeper into child custody, spousal support, property division, and finalization, offering a road map for the journey ahead.

Additionally, I'll provide strategies to help you navigate the emotional and practical challenges that arise as you transition to a new chapter in your life.

CHAPTER 5
Working with Your Lawyer

In Chapter 3, we established that you do, indeed, need representation for your divorce case. You may have even followed the guidelines we provided and hired an attorney. Part of me wants to offer congratulations (because that's a crucial first step), and part of me wants to offer condolences, because . . . well, it's a divorce.

In this chapter, we're going to cover what happens next and how to work with your attorney to ensure that they have the tools they need to give you the most value for your money. It's been my experience that the savviest lawyers often have the savviest clients. By this, I don't mean you need any legal acumen (quite the contrary); rather, I'm talking about clients who are willing to roll up their sleeves and go the extra mile to provide the communication and, yes, documentation that enable your attorney to advance your case with an absolute minimum of guesswork and even fewer surprises.

Neither lawyers nor judges like surprises. The only surprise should be on the part of your ex and their attorney at just how prepared your attorney is.

 HOW TO BE A SAVVY DIVORCE CLIENT

Gather Ye Records

Just as in a criminal trial, cases are made or lost on the weight of evidence; in a divorce case, that's exactly what your financial records are. Start pulling together tax returns, bank statements (both checking and savings), retirement account and life insurance statements, home mortgage loans, credit card statements, pay stubs . . . if it's related to finances, you'll need it. Start with the most recent and work backward. Keep in mind that at some point you'll have to put a dollar figure to everything of value you own.

You don't necessarily need to gather all of these documents at the very outset; for one thing, many of them will be updated throughout. Your attorney will provide guidance as to exactly what he or she needs—and when—as your case progresses. That being said, the more information you can gather early, the more time you'll save down the road.

Keep a Journal

This can be especially important in cases involving children, and even more so if there are disputes in that area. It doesn't have to be overly detailed, just record anything that relates to where the kids are staying, what's going on in their lives, and what the other party is doing. As you might imagine, this journal usually won't be given any weight as actual evidence in court—as you're one of the parties involved, an element of bias in your account of events is unavoidable. However, it does give you a record to testify from so that you're not forgetting important details. Writing things down contemporaneously (as they're happening) only adds credibility. Emailing your journal entries to yourself (thereby creating a timestamp) provides even more credibility.

Communicate via Email

Speaking of timestamps, once your divorce case is proceeding, I highly recommend you limit your communications—as much as is practically possible—to emails. While both emails and texts provide timestamps for when the communications took place, texts are tougher to present. They often require screenshots of conversation threads that paint a less concise (and more confusing) picture of what's going on.

Obviously, there will be times when a telephone conversation is unavoidable. *Don't record these calls!* In the very best-case scenario, those recordings are worthless in court. In the worst case—if your state happens to have two-party consent laws for recording telephone conversations—you'll have committed a felony. That definitely doesn't help your case. Your best bet is to follow up your phone call with an email, covering the main points of what was discussed and how (or whether) the particular topic was resolved.

And please—keep your written correspondence with your ex (or their attorneys) civil and professional. Stick to the facts, follow a consistent format in your emails, and don't get emotional. You don't want timestamped documentation showing the judge your proficiency with profanity. Pretend you're CC-ing your grandmother. (Note: There's usually no need to CC your grandmother.)

Organize Your Records

As you present all of this paperwork to your lawyer, keep in mind that time is money. Even if you've hired a fixed-fee attorney, forcing them to waste hours organizing all of your evidence isn't an efficient use of their time. Don't throw everything into a binder labeled "Divorce Stuff" and dump it on your attorney's desk. (Don't laugh. I've seen variations of this multiple times.)

Think of each piece of your documentation as an individual piece of evidence—because that's what it is. Treat it that way. Arrange your financial records in a logical and systematic order, perhaps using labeled folders or tabs. Regarding your journals and communication records, organize them chronologically, with each email on a separate page, so that your attorney actually has a timeline of events at their fingertips.

This methodical approach not only demonstrates your commitment to presenting a coherent case but also ensures that your attorney can navigate through the information with ease, ultimately contributing to a more compelling and organized presentation during your divorce proceedings.

Honestly? Be Honest!

Everything your attorney has in their arsenal as your legal representative hinges on the degree to which you are—or aren't—completely, 100 percent, open and honest in your communication with them about your case. You're paying this person to be your advisor and your guide. Failing to provide them with all the tools and information they need to best represent you is *not* the way to go!

In any divorce case, especially those with children involved, there are very few aspects of your personal and professional life that won't be factors in the outcome.

Withholding pertinent information about a new romantic partner or a DUI you'd like to keep on the hush-hush can severely compromise your lawyer's ability to formulate a strategy to mitigate any potential damage to your case. Keeping silent and crossing your fingers that your ex or their counsel doesn't find out (and you should assume they most definitely will) can leave your attorney on the ropes and leave both of you looking like idiots.

This same principle applies to your assets. It's quite common for clients to think they can put one over on their ex by finding clever ways to hide assets. Don't be tempted—there's too much at risk. Credibility will play a huge role in the way the judge looks at your case; any lies or flagrant attempts at obfuscating the truth can cause the judge to apply a skeptical inference to every aspect of your case, beyond just the particular issue or issues that you were less than honest about.

Be clear and upfront with your attorney about what's important to you. Certain aspects of issues, such as spousal support, child custody, or division of assets, may not be as important to you as others. The same will probably be true of your ex. Making sure your attorney is aware of the things that are most important to *you* helps them negotiate with an element of leverage.

Your priorities can—and often will—evolve as your case moves forward. Say you're a divorcing mother with school-age kids. At the beginning, you may think keeping the house and not disrupting your children's lives is a "must-have." Time may change your outlook. You may come to decide that the financial commitment required isn't the best route for you to take and that the benefits of downsizing outweigh the benefits of staying put.

Another common example of priorities evolving with a case involves spousal support. Even though your ex was the primary breadwinner in the relationship, you're intent on exerting your independence. You can do it on your own; you don't need your ex's money. As time passes, however, you may realize that a somewhat softer landing would be, well, nice, and that some spousal support might be the best way to make that happen.

In either event, *tell your lawyer.* There's a very good chance they've been pursuing a strategy based on your original priorities. They'll need to adjust.

DIFFERENCE BETWEEN LEGAL AND
NONLEGAL ISSUES IN A DIVORCE

Distinguish between Legal and Nonlegal

Understanding the distinction between legal and nonlegal issues in your divorce case is paramount for navigating the complexities of the legal process effectively. Legal issues pertain directly to matters governed by the law, such as asset division, child custody, spousal support, and any other legally binding agreements. These aspects involve court proceedings, legal standards, and the application of statutes to ensure a fair and just resolution.

On the other hand, nonlegal issues encompass a broader spectrum of personal and emotional considerations that may impact the divorce process but may not fall strictly within the confines of legal statutes. Emotional well-being, communication challenges, and co-parenting dynamics are examples of nonlegal issues that can significantly influence the overall divorce experience. While your attorney may offer guidance for managing these nonlegal aspects, they often involve collaborative efforts with therapists, mediators, or other professionals outside the legal realm.

Listen to Your Lawyer

You're paying your attorney to provide sound legal advice and help you pursue the best—or at least the most painless—resolution to your divorce. Take their advice.

Often clients can be so emotionally charged about an issue that they simply don't want to hear anything that doesn't comport with their preconceived notions. They don't like the advice they're given, so they fight it. In the worst cases, they fire their lawyer and hire one that will tell them what they want to hear. That's a good recipe for an unsatisfying result.

If you're going to hire a lawyer, at least *listen* to that lawyer. They're not there to give you a bad outcome. You may feel like you want certain things, but the sad fact is that sometimes what you want just isn't feasible; your attorney knows from experience that the court isn't going to grant it. Your lawyer's job is to help you see that and understand that there will have to be some compromise. You're simply not going to get every single thing you're asking for. A good lawyer will help you strike a balance between what you want and what it's *possible* to get. They're on your side. Listen to them.

Ignore Legal Advice from Family and Friends

It's sad that in America today, virtually everyone either has gone through divorce or is close to someone who has. That doesn't mean they know anything about divorce *law*.

Your family and friends love you. They want to help you put an end to the pain. And when it comes to providing emotional support throughout your ordeal, they're perfect for that. But they're most likely not attorneys. Even the ones that are attorneys are probably not divorce attorneys. If they are—and if they check off all the boxes in chapter 3—well, you've probably already hired them. Otherwise, their advice is best left ignored.

And resist the temptation to bring your "posse" with you to meetings with your lawyer. Even if your parents or siblings are helping you with the costs of your divorce, they're not entitled to be privy to your attorney consultations. Your lawyer is *your* lawyer, no matter who's footing the bill.

Pay Your Attorney

This one sounds like a no-brainer, but you would be surprised at how many clients fail to make it a priority. Timely payment of your divorce lawyer is essential for fostering a productive and effective working relationship throughout the process. Legal services take considerable time, expertise, and resources, and prompt payment demonstrates your commitment to the professional partnership. Consistent and punctual payments allow your attorney to focus on advocating for your interests rather than dealing with financial matters. This reliability also helps build trust and mutual respect, reinforcing a positive working dynamic. In turn, a financially sound and transparent relationship ensures that your attorney can dedicate their full attention to navigating the complexities of your case, ultimately enhancing the likelihood of a favorable outcome in your divorce proceedings.

Obviously, there are no surefire tips for getting the very best resolution to your divorce. Following the guidelines above, however, can help ensure that you and your attorney are working together with maximum synchronicity and efficiency. Being a savvy client is the very best way to facilitate the very best results and can give you a distinct, strategic edge—especially if your ex hasn't read this book!

CHAPTER 6
Child Custody

In the complex landscape of divorce, perhaps no issue is more contentious and fraught with emotion than child custody. Any good parent knows that, as tough as divorce is on the splitting spouses, their heartache doesn't hold a candle to the devastating impact divorce can have on their children. After all, in many—if not most—cases, these kids have never known a reality in which Mommy and Daddy aren't together.

Children are the ultimate innocent bystanders.

In this chapter, we'll cover what every divorcing parent needs to know about child custody:

- The distinctions between legal custody and physical custody (sometimes called "placement," "visitation," or "parenting time").

- How custody battles can be a perfect storm of emotional anxiety for the kids, and signs you need to watch out for.

- Strategies for getting the best results in a custody battle.

- The Eight Commandments of Parenting for divorcing parents.

- How to prepare for trial on child custody issues.

- The best-interest standards that judges and courts will apply to those issues.

LEGAL CUSTODY VS.
PHYSICAL CUSTODY

Legal Custody vs. Physical Custody

In divorce proceedings for cases with children involved, *legal custody* and *physical custody* (or an aforementioned variation of physical custody) refer to different aspects of the parent-child relationship. Parents going through divorce often talk as if the terms are somewhat interchangeable, thinking of custody in the context of physical possession. That's not really how it works.

Legal custody is the authority to make major decisions in a child's life, such as those related to education, healthcare, and religion. The parent with sole legal custody has the final say on such issues. This type of custody arrangement is usually reserved for cases in which the relationship between the parents is just so acrimonious, or one parent is so unfit, that giving all the legal decision-making power to one parent is in the best interests of the child (or children).

Joint legal custody is, in my experience, by far the most common arrangement. Courts always want what's in the best interests of the child, and that usually means allowing both parents to continue sharing in major decisions. Most courts start with a presumption of joint legal custody.

There are also certain hybrid legal custody arrangements (often known as "split" or "divided" legal custody) in which parents are allocated specific areas of decision-making authority or responsibility for the child. For example, one parent may have the authority to make decisions about the child's education, while the other has decision-making authority over the child's health care. This approach aims to capitalize on each parent's strengths and involvement in specific aspects of the child's life. In my experience, these arrangements are quite rare.

Physical custody pertains to where the child primarily resides. The parent with physical custody is responsible for the day-to-day care of the child. *Placement* refers to the schedule or plan that outlines when the noncustodial parent (the one without primary physical custody) has the right to spend time with the child. It delineates the specific periods during which the noncustodial parent can have access to and responsibility for the child. The most common form of placement—and the one that, if you were a child of divorce, you probably recognize—is some variation of the traditional "every other weekend, two weeks in the summer, and alternate major holidays" arrangement.

Another type of physical custody arrangement which—though not common—happens more than you might think, is sometimes called a *nesting arrangement*. In this scenario, the children remain in the home and the parents take turns living there. As you might imagine, this type of arrangement is rarely long-term; in my experience, it's used mostly during protracted, ongoing divorce cases.

You've probably heard the old adage "Possession is nine-tenths of the law." In divorce cases, this doesn't necessarily apply. If you and your ex have joint *legal* custody, any decision that falls into the realm of legal custody (as outlined above), even during "your time" with the kids, still requires the approval of your ex.

HOW A CUSTODY BATTLE
AFFECTS YOUR KIDS

A Perfect Storm: The Effects of a Custody Battle on Your Kids

The idea of causing our children emotional harm runs contrary to everything we try to do as parents. Sadly, in the heat of a divorce, far too many parents seem to forget this basic tenet of parenting and engage in protracted custody battles.

They tell themselves it's "for the children," but that's rarely the case. In fact, if you want to ensure that your kids will suffer long-term psychological effects—a perfect storm of anxiety, stress, and depression—as a result of your divorce, a vicious battle with your ex over custody is a good way to do it.

Kids don't like to see their parents fighting. It only exacerbates their profound feelings of instability at a time when they're overwhelmed by them already. They didn't sign on for this upheaval in their lives. More than anything, at this time, they need to be able to hold on to some semblance of certainty, of *normalcy*. They need to know where they're going to live and whom they're going to live with. They need to be assured that their parents still love them, even if they no longer seem to love each other.

They *don't* need to be innocent casualties of war, forced to go through humiliating evaluations, to "take sides" with one parent, or to bare their souls for a guardian or other third party they don't even know (which we'll cover later).

One of the most heart-wrenching aspects of my job is seeing these young lives come unraveled as kids live out their worst nightmares. It doesn't have to be like this. If you want what's best for your child's happiness and emotional well-being, it *shouldn't* be like this.

During this emotional roller coaster ride for your children, be vigilant for signs of psychological trauma. Look for changes in sleeping or eating habits, bouts of depression or volatile mood swings, a marked decline in their performance at school, and/or a sudden lack of interest in extracurricular activities. All of these can be symptoms of emotional trauma that may need a professional's attention.

HOW TO GET THE BEST OUTCOME IN A CUSTODY BATTLE

Custody Battle Strategies

As much as you may want to avoid a custody battle, sometimes it's just not possible. After all, custody is a two-way street, and your ex may have demands that you truly believe aren't in the best interests of your children. If you find yourself in this unfortunate situation, these are some basic strategies you can enlist to help your attorney be at their most effective.

Be on Your Best Behavior

In divorce cases with children involved, it's crucial to realize that your behavior is going to be under the microscope. One of the key players is the neutral guardian—such as a guardian *ad litem* (GAL) or child advocate attorney—appointed by the court to represent the best interests of the child. They investigate and assess the child's living conditions, relationships, and overall well-being.

They'll be watching. The judge will be watching. Social workers will be watching. Therapists may be watching. All of these folks—particularly the guardian—can stand between you and the resolution to your case.

Don't misbehave. Be courteous, be on time for everything, and be polite and professional in all your exchanges and communications, not just with the abovementioned professionals but with your ex and your children.

Be Present with Your Children

There may have been times before all this started when you weren't able to go to one of your child's functions. You may have missed the occasional soccer match or music recital or parent-teacher conference.

Don't miss any of those now. Whether it takes missing a work meeting or moving a mountain, *be there*. Again, people are watching. The more accommodating and involved you are with your kids' lives during this time, the better it will serve your interests in the long run.

At the same time, keep in mind that you can be *too* present. Don't badger your kids into doing things they don't want to do just for the appearance of "presence." The bottom line is that you want to build an inviting, welcoming, safe, emotionally warm place for them. Don't make them uncomfortable by doting on them too much. If you've got a strained relationship with a child (usually more common with older kids), a sudden attempt to repair that relationship might seem suspicious to them. Obviously, you'll be making an ongoing effort to make things right; just don't overdo it.

Double Up on Supplies

Speaking of accommodating the kids, if you and your spouse are already living separately (and you're the noncustodial parent), bite the bullet and buy new sets of clothes and new toys for your children. Buy new beds for them. If they've got a bicycle at home, buy them a bicycle for *your* home. The more you can reduce the anxiety of this life-changing transition for them, the more you show the court, your GAL, and of course your kids how much you prioritize their happiness.

Get Used to Saying "Our Kids"

This one may seem kind of trivial, but I assure you it most definitely is not. One almost surefire way to raise red flags in the minds of judges, guardians, and other court officials is to refer to your children in a possessive way, especially if it's exclusionary of the other parent. Remember, these folks hold many aspects of your future with your children in their hands; referring to your kids as "*my* kids" signals to them a hesitancy toward the collaboration and cooperation with the other parent that serves the best interests of the child.

When I said earlier that your behavior is going to be under a microscope, this is a good example of what I meant. Even words (and *small* words at that) matter.

Stay off Social Media

For parents not active on Facebook or Instagram or TikTok or X, this one's easy. If you're among the huge number of parents, however, who are active on social media, it may seem like I just asked you to amputate a limb.

You can do it (stay off social media, not amputate). I know that social media is how many people stay connected to the world. It's where they celebrate their happiness and vent their frustration.

If this is you, *stop it*. I literally cannot count the number of times I've seen clients shoot themselves in the foot by venting about their divorce (or engaging in activity that casts them in a negative light) on social media. Even if you don't have children, it's a good idea to stay unplugged. If you do have kids, it's imperative.

If you have enough self-control to limit your posts to cute videos of puppies and the like, you might be okay. Just always keep it in the front of your mind that everything you share online can be shared in court. If it's anything—anything at all—that could somehow be detrimental to your case, it will be. If you have to vent, vent to your attorney. Vent to your therapist. Vent (privately) to your close friends. Don't vent to the world!

THE EIGHT COMMANDMENTS OF PARENTING DURING A DIVORCE

The Eight Commandments of Parenting during Divorce

As I've mentioned (and worthy of repeated emphasis), these are the times during which your parenting will be under the strictest scrutiny. Some of these commandments will apply even if you don't have kids.

I. Thou shalt follow court orders

Typically, after one party files for divorce, a "temporary order" is put in place that outlines the rules until the final decree is issued. Now's not the time to violate any of those rules.

II. Thou shalt not badmouth or trash-talk thy spouse to thy children

Just don't. Your kids love *both* of you. The psychological damage you can inflict on these innocent bystanders by constantly putting down or demonizing their other parent can last a lifetime.

III. Thou shalt not use thy children as messengers

Look, your kids are already inextricably involved in your divorce. That doesn't mean you should get them more involved. If you have something to say to your spouse, *you* say it (or, better yet—as we discussed in the last chapter—email it). Keep the children out of it.

IV. Thou shalt not ask thy children which parent they want to live with

The decision of which parent they want to live with during a divorce is another burden your kids can do without. You're forcing them to pick sides, which can harm their relationship with both of you. Your kids are already experiencing guilt and anxiety they've never known before; asking them to make such a weighty decision only adds to it.

V. Thou shalt keep thy household rules consistent

It can be tempting to try to curry favor with your kids by relaxing long-established household rules (like "No TV/video games until homework's done") during their time with you. Resist this temptation. At its core, this is either bribery or a childish attempt at antagonizing your spouse. In either case, it's counterproductive to the stability that your children most need right now.

VI. Thou shalt not give thy children false hope

It can be heartbreaking when your child (especially a young child) asks, "When's Daddy coming home?" or "When are you and Mommy going to make up?" Every instinct you have as a parent compels you to try to placate or console them. Yet, by giving them false hope, you're just setting them up for more confusion and heartache down the road. This isn't to say you need to be brutally honest. There's no reason to answer any of the above questions with some variation of "When hell freezes over" (see Commandment II).

VII. Thou shalt keep thy children informed— but not too informed

Of course, unless they're infants or toddlers, your kids are going to know that you and your spouse are getting a divorce, and it's okay to give them the basic "headlines" of what's going on in the case. There's no need, however, to let them in on every little detail. Chances are they don't want to know that stuff. And there's a good chance that telling them about all the behind-the-scenes wrangling and machinations will only add to their anxiety.

VIII. Thou shalt not use thy children as thy therapist
Your kids are going through enough right now. They don't need to also be burdened with just how unhappy or angry you are. Keep your boundaries.

 WHAT IS THE BEST-INTEREST STANDARD IN A CUSTODY DISPUTE?

Best-Interest Standards

Ideally, you'll be able to negotiate an arrangement with your spouse for child custody and placement. That's almost always the best way to go; it's definitely the least costly—both financially and emotionally.

Unfortunately, it just doesn't work sometimes. There may be elements that your ex is "dug in" on, or there may be things you're unwilling to compromise. It happens.

In those cases, it'll be up to the judge.

If you find yourself in court, standing up for your rights as a parent, it's crucial to be completely candid and specific about your parenting strengths/weaknesses. Obviously, the first part's easy; the second part is where people run into trouble. Understand that there are very few things about you that your spouse's attorney (and, hence, the judge) won't know.

Maybe, as the primary breadwinner of the family, you weren't as involved in your child's day-to-day life as you would have liked. Own it. Whatever you do, don't get defensive about it. Rather, be forthright and explain the specific steps you'll take to remedy the situation.

By the same token, you should be able to articulate your spouse's parenting strengths and weaknesses. In this case, it'll be far easier for you to pinpoint the weaknesses, but don't hesitate to give credit where credit's due. And—regarding your ex's weaknesses—don't use this as an opportunity to badmouth them. Remain calm and reasoned, and always keep in mind that rumors and innuendo don't work in court.

You should also be able to demonstrate to the judge an awareness of virtually every detail of your child's life and routines, from the time they wake up to get ready for school to their schedules for meals and extracurricular activities. You need to show that you have a plan for ensuring their routines won't be unduly disrupted. Know who their friends are, who their teachers are. Show that you have a specific plan, if required, for adjusting your work schedule to meet all of your child's needs.

In most states, to decide who gets custody of the kids following a divorce, judges adhere to what are known as "best-interest standards." These standards are basically a way of figuring out what's best for the child rather than favoring one parent over the other. As you can probably guess, no two situations are exactly alike.

The judge looks at various factors, like the child's age, health, and any special needs; how mentally and physically fit each parent is; the home environment; the child's relationship with each parent; and whether the parents can create a good and supportive atmosphere.

They also consider the willingness and ability of each parent to facilitate a healthy and ongoing relationship between the child and the other parent. The aim is to promote a sense of continuity and stability in the child's life, enabling them to maintain a connection with both parents whenever feasible. Courts may also assess factors such as the child's adjustment to their community, school, and surroundings, emphasizing the importance of mini-mizing disruption to the child's established routines.

As I've said before (and as I'll no doubt say again), divorce is tough. If you have children, it's even tougher. There are no winners, least of all the only completely innocent parties in your breakup. Your lawyer's job is to make it all as painless as possible.

Understanding exactly what's involved in ensuring that your rights as a parent are upheld and following the suggestions above will go a long way toward helping your attorney to do just that.

CHAPTER 7
Financial Support

When the nightmare that is divorce finally winds its way through the legal process, after you've paid your attorney's and other court-related fees, and after the dust has somewhat settled and you're able to hopefully start getting on with your new life, you're still likely going to either face years of financial commitment to your ex-spouse and (if applicable) your children or be due that commitment from your ex.

And most agree that there's really nothing wrong with this. The conflict that often arises, of course, is just a matter of numbers: how much, how often, and for how long. In this chapter, we're going to break down what you need to know about child support and "maintenance" (often known as *spousal support* or *alimony*). We'll talk about guidelines for child support and how long it will have to be paid, how courts determine the income used to set a dollar amount, how medical and college experiences factor into the equation, and related tax ramifications.

Regarding maintenance, we'll cover different types of payment arrangements, some recent trends among jurisdictions, and the factors the courts look at when setting a dollar amount. We'll also take a look at prenuptial agreements, or "prenups," and the impact they have (or often don't have) on the court's decision.

HOW CHILD SUPPORT WORKS
IN A DIVORCE

Child Support

Let's first talk about the kids.

Federal law mandates that every state establish child support guidelines. Now, it's important to understand that when we talk about these guidelines, they're not rigid, strict, or absolute. They're not "etched in stone," as it were. Courts have a degree of discretion—especially in cases involving significant income disparities or high earners—allowing them to deviate slightly from the established guidelines.

How Much?

Usually these guidelines operate on a percentage-based system, factoring in each party's income and the time they spend with the child to formulate a support amount. Unfortunately, this approach can lead to uneven and seemingly unfair outcomes, and it often becomes a major point of contention between the parties, masquerading as a custody and placement dispute.

Why? Because both parties (or at least their lawyers) are aware that—once a resolution is reached on time allocation—child support inevitably follows, leaving little room for negotiation.

Many states employ the *income shares* method to determine child support, adhering to the concept that a child's share of the total parental income should remain unaffected by the divorce. The underlying principle is to mitigate the financial impact on the child and ensure continued financial support and care.

This method can seem unfair in some situations. For instance, when one parent has less time with the child (e.g., 35 percent for the dad and 65 percent for the mom), the child support payments may disproportionately burden the parent with less time. The discrepancy arises when the financial obligation surpasses the incremental cost of additional expenses incurred by the custodial parent, like buying extra food. In plain English, this means the money one parent has to pay for child support is more than the extra money the parent taking care of the child actually has to spend.

Despite the perceived (and often actual) unfairness, a more equitable solution remains a tough nut to crack, and it makes these calculations and applications of child support methods seem more complex and weirder than they might need to be.

As if all this isn't complex and weird enough already, in some states, child support calculations may include additional expenses like health insurance and childcare costs, increasing the overall support amount ordered by the court. As I mentioned, courts do have the authority to deviate from standard guidelines, but it's usually challenging to meet the high burdens required for such deviations. The court may consider future bonuses, employment perks, and certain deductions from the parent's income (like mandatory pension contributions or union dues). However, some factors—like being in a union—are beyond the parent's control; that may be taken into account.

How Long?

As with many elements of divorce law, the duration of required child support varies among states and lacks consistency. Generally, child support extends until the child turns eighteen or graduates from high school, whichever comes later (typically around the age of nineteen). This time frame holds as long as the child continues to pursue high school education or its equivalent. Again, this standard could be different in your jurisdiction. Your attorney will be able to tell you for certain.

Determining Income

When it comes to determining income for child support considerations, it's not just about a straightforward base income. Various financial elements come into play, including bonuses, commissions, and overtime. Courts may even consider perks such as a company car or reimbursements for personal items, though these allowances are subject to debate. The objective is to assess the *total benefit* received by the individual, accounting for both monetary and nonmonetary contributions.

When dealing with a self-employed spouse or business owner, the complexity only intensifies. In these cases, the total benefit encompasses not only salary but also personal bills covered by the business—perks like leased vehicles and any factors affecting the business's bottom line, such as deductions, depreciation, taxes, and retained earnings. Does this often lead to even more disputes and litigation? I'll bet you can guess the answer to that one (Hint: It's yes).

Child support is also distinctive in that the government has a vested interest in ensuring adequate care for the child. After all, it's the government that may have to step in if one party neglects their payment responsibilities, placing a burden on public resources.

Child Support and Taxes

It's important to note that the money you pay for child support is post-tax, meaning you can't claim it as a deduction. In Wisconsin, for instance, child support payments are calculated at 17 percent of your gross income if you have one child. This means for someone making $100,000 annually and paying support for a single kid, after paying child support and somewhere around 30 percent for state and federal taxes, they'll have about 53 percent of their salary to live on.

Again, that's for one child. If you have two, that rate goes up to 25 percent. If you have five kids or more (as I do), a $100,000 annual income—after state and federal taxes and 34 percent for child support—becomes approximately $36,000 in "take-home" pay.

There *is* a silver lining, just not for the parent paying the support. If you're the custodial parent, the child support money you receive is not considered taxable income. So there's that.

Now you might better understand why child custody and support can get so contentious—and why it's absolutely crucial you have an experienced attorney on your side.

What's at Stake?

One of the only things that can be more financially impactful than paying child support, at least within

this particular area of divorce, is *not* paying it. Falling
into arrears on your court-ordered support can open up
a can of worms that puts all your other legal costs to
shame. With sky-high interest rates (often around 12–18
percent), this can be an ongoing debt that usually can't be
relieved even through bankruptcy without the approval
of your former spouse. You could literally be paying off
your child support until long after your kids have turned
eighteen. You could be paying it off until your *grandkids*
turn eighteen. It's just one of many good reasons to avoid
becoming a lifelong sworn enemy of your ex.

Perhaps now you understand why I said earlier that
if you're getting a divorce and you have children, a good
lawyer is a must-have.

HOW ALIMONY WORKS IN
DIVORCE COURT

Maintenance

Besides child support, there's support for your former
spouse. Terms like *spousal support, maintenance,* and
alimony are highly interchangeable, with minor variations in their definitions from state to state. While some
states may use different terms, they essentially refer to
the same concept. *Alimony* has historically been the most
recognized term—the one most often heard on TV at

least—but, in contemporary legal language, most states prefer the other two. For the sake of simplicity, I'll just use *maintenance* from here on out.

How Much?

When determining maintenance, several key factors come into play. In my experience, the most important one is the duration of the marriage. For short-term marriages, courts may lean toward limited support, assuming less financial entanglement. In mid-term marriages, they might consider a transitional approach, helping the bene-fiting spouse attain financial independence. Long-term marriages often result in higher amounts of maintenance, reflecting the deep economic ties of the spouses.

The second crucial factor is the combined income of both parties, including *all* income sources (not just wages). This number is determined using many of the same criteria we discussed in the previous section. The court also considers the age and health of the individuals, along with any specific needs beyond routine day-to-day requirements.

Another aspect the court may evaluate is whether one spouse needs more education or training to become more employable. Assessing whether they can get a better job post-education is key here. Childcare responsibilities also factor in, with the court examining whether one party shoulders more of the day-to-day care.

One somewhat perplexing factor is the standard of living during the marriage. While some (including me) may question its relevance post-divorce, courts often use it as a basis for their decisions. The division of assets and liabilities (which we'll cover in the next chapter) is also crucial; if the recipient spouse receives a large portion of the estate, monthly support may be less imperative.

Tax implications for both parties are taken into account, adding another layer of complexity to the assessment. Courts often consider all relevant aspects of the tax situation with some sort of "catch-all" provision for any other pertinent factors.

It's worth noting that in some states, courts may also look at marital misconduct. Not all jurisdictions give it much weight (Wisconsin and Illinois, for example, don't), but in some southern states, it can play a role in the amount of maintenance owed.

How Long?

Nationally, the trend in recent times (thanks in part to legislative efforts) leans toward shorter durations for maintenance than in times past—a departure from lifetime maintenance. While Wisconsin lacks a strict rule, a common guideline is that beyond twenty years, maintenance becomes indefinite; some counties may draw the line at fifteen years. Your lawyer will be able to tell you for sure (or at least they really should be able to; see chapter 3).

It's essential to clarify, however, that "indefinite" doesn't mean a guaranteed lifetime commitment. The courts generally don't set an end date, leaving it to the parties to revisit the issue in the future. Termination triggers may include remarriage, retirement, or a specific retirement age.

There's also the possibility, in some cases, of a "lump sum" arrangement for maintenance, meaning one party just pays a fixed amount up front. These types of arrangements aren't usually ordered by the courts; instead, both parties agree to them after negotiations.

As very few states employ a fixed formula for setting maintenance obligations (either the amount or the length), judicial decisions can vary greatly. Some states are gradually moving toward providing clearer guidelines or formulas to help judges apply the law more evenly. In Wisconsin and Illinois, for example, counties often have "unspoken rules" known only to seasoned attorneys; you can have inconsistencies not just from one jurisdiction to another, but even among individual judges within the same county.

All of these are reasons you should have an experienced attorney who knows your jurisdiction and how the judges there tend to work.

HOW A PRENUPTIAL
AGREEMENT WORKS

Prenuptial Agreements

A prenup—a written agreement made between you and your spouse at the time (or just before) you get married—can be tricky. While designed to provide clarity and protection if divorce happens, they may (or may not) be worth the paper they're written on. When well-drafted and carried out properly, a prenuptial agreement can serve as a legally binding document that outlines how assets will be split, the terms of maintenance, and other key matters. It offers a level of certainty and prevents long disputes during a divorce.

However, there's no guarantee that a prenup will be enforced, and challenges can (and almost certainly will) arise. Courts may scrutinize the circumstances under which the agreement was made, looking for signs of coercion, duress, or lack of full disclosure. If the agreement is deemed unfair or unconscionable, or if one party did not have adequate legal representation, it may be deemed invalid. Also, changes in circumstances during the marriage, such as the birth of children, major financial changes, or failure to update the agreement, can lead to disputes over whether the prenup can be enforced.

A good attorney—one who not only knows divorce law but knows how the local family court judges view prenups—can tell you whether you've got an ironclad agreement or just a piece of paper.

CHAPTER 8
Property Division

HOW PROPERTY DIVISION WORKS
IN A DIVORCE

If you've been married for any length of time, you and your spouse have probably accumulated "stuff." This could be stuff like a house and cars and the debts you incurred while getting that house and those cars. In fact, it could be anything of value that you or your spouse bought while you were married. Depending on how old you were when you got married, you may have had plenty of stuff even before that.

So, when you divorce, who gets all that stuff?

In this chapter, I'm going to tell you what you need to know about property division. We'll unpack concepts like marital vs. nonmarital property, how debts are allocated, which property and assets get divided and which don't, and the myriad factors courts look at—including whether a state is guided by "equitable distribution" or "community property" regulations—when deciding who gets what.

We'll also look at assets like closely held businesses and professional practices and the appraisals and other factors used by courts to determine their value.

Finally, we'll cover how retirement plans are often divided and the tax implications of property division.

As you've probably already guessed, this stuff can sometimes get pretty complex—just one more reason why, if you and your spouse have any significant property or other assets, you really need to have a good attorney on your side.

Laws Governing Property Division

In general, most states adhere to the concept of equitable division of property, emphasizing fairness in the distribution of assets. However, a handful of states—around ten or twelve, including Wisconsin—operate under the community property model, in which a fifty-fifty split is the starting presumption. This fundamental difference is a big one.

Under equitable division, the court considers various factors—such as the duration of the marriage, each spouse's financial contributions to particular assets, and individual needs—to arrive at a division deemed, as the name implies, equitable. This method allows for a more flexible and personalized distribution of assets, acknowledging the unique circumstances of each case.

For instance, the duration of the marriage is a crucial consideration. A longer marriage might warrant a more even distribution, as the contributions and entwined (or "commingled," as we lawyers like to say) financial affairs over an extended period often make a clear fifty-fifty division equitable. On the other hand, in shorter marriages, the court may lean toward a distribution that reflects each spouse's individual contributions during the marriage.

In equitable division states, financial contributions to specific assets—including, of course, the family home—play a pivotal role. If one spouse contributed a lot more to buy or improve the property, the court may adjust the distribution to recognize that financial input.

But that's not all: The courts in equitable division states also consider individual needs and circumstances. A classic example is when the spouse with primary custody of the children is awarded a larger share of the family home. To most, this seems like the equitable thing to do—you know, for the kids.

Again, if you're in one of all but a handful of states, these are the issues you and your attorney (and your spouse and his or her attorney) will be grappling with.

On the other hand, community property states presume assets and property are jointly owned, with each spouse entitled to an equal share. Obviously, this approach is simpler, but unless you've been married for a long time, it probably doesn't seem quite so . . . well, equitable.

This isn't to say there aren't exceptions to this "split down the middle" rule: In short-term marriages (lasting five years or less), the courts typically aim to restore each party to their pre-marital financial position, particularly when there are no children involved. So even states following community property guidelines still aim for at least some fairness and equity.

Just as in equitable division states, as the length of the marriage extends, the likelihood of recovering premarital assets diminishes. In other words, the chance of being restored to your premarital financial condition becomes less and less likely the longer you're married. If you've been married twenty years or more, even if you can clearly trace your contribution to the purchase of a particular asset, it's probably not going to make much of a difference.

What Gets Divided: Marital vs. Nonmarital Property

Whether you're in a community property state or an equitable division state, not everything gets divvied up.

Marital property encompasses assets and debts acquired by either spouse during the marriage. It includes income earned, real estate purchased, personal property acquired, and debts incurred from the start of the marriage until the date of separation or divorce. (Note: Different jurisdictions may define the "end of the marriage" as either the date of separation, the divorce filing date, or the date when the court issues the final divorce decree.) This typically means the family home, vehicles, joint bank accounts, and any other assets acquired jointly during the marriage are divided, whether equitably or fifty-fifty.

What won't be eligible for the "chopping block" is nonmarital property, or assets that either spouse owned before the marriage or acquired during the marriage through inheritance, gift, or specific exclusion. As mentioned earlier, however, commingling of nonmarital property with marital assets (especially in longer-term marriages) can sometimes complicate things.

Dividing Debts

Any debts you and your spouse rack up during your marriage will most likely be viewed as shared responsibilities and divided accordingly. The court will basically make a list of everything you both own and owe, divvy it up, and try to make it fair.

It's super important to note that credit card companies don't care about—nor do they have to abide by—your divorce agreement. Divorce papers don't magically protect you from creditors, and in most states, creditors will go after the person who owes them money, no matter what the divorce papers say. The exception to this is in community property states, where creditors might chase both of you.

To avoid post-divorce money headaches, it's a good idea to settle debts before the divorce is finalized.

Factors in Dividing Property

Most states—around two-thirds—have laws on the books listing the factors that the courts can consider when determining property division. In other states, they rely on precedent from previous cases. In virtually all cases, each judge decides how much weight to give each of these factors.

As a general rule, they'll look at the ages of you and your spouse, any health issues either of you may have, and the length of the marriage. They'll also consider the children you have together and their ages, as well as the lifestyle the family enjoys. They're going to factor in the education, occupation, and earning capacity of you and your ex and your prospects for the future.

Many judges look at misconduct, especially if it's related to the current divorce proceedings. You may have heard of somebody going through a divorce who blows a huge wad of cash or signs over assets to a boyfriend or girlfriend or family member to keep their spouse from getting any of it. A judge may be able to hold that against you. In some cases, a prosecutor might too!

Some states may even allow judges to weigh infidelity in their property division decisions. This happens only in what are known as "fault" states, where the actual reasons for the divorce can play a role in the court's decision. As you might guess, this is in contrast to the "no-fault" states, which don't really care what caused the breakup. A few states are even a combination of both.

In case you're wondering, there is no correlation between "no-fault" divorce laws and "no-fault" insurance laws. Just because your state has one doesn't mean it has the other.

The Marital Residence

For many divorcing couples, their home is their most valuable asset. It's also an asset with all sorts of practical and logistical implications, especially if you have children. I've already told you the role equitable division and community property laws will have when it comes to divvying up the house (rest assured that—regardless of which of these your state follows—there will be no chainsaws involved), and some of the other factors courts may weigh when making their decisions. But let's look at a few practical and logistical matters that can also play a role.

- **Residential arrangements:** In some cases—especially those with kids—one party may want to continue living in the home. As I've mentioned, courts will always strive to prioritize the welfare and stability of the children, but they'll also weigh factors such as child custody agreements and financial capabilities in their decision.

- **Financial obligations:** Unless you and your spouse decide to sell the home (which happens often when there are no kids involved), there will be ongoing costs, like mortgage payments and property taxes. Who pays what percentage of those costs will be an issue for negotiation or judgement.

- **Buyout option:** Often one spouse will choose to keep the home and buy out the other's equity.

This can require its own set of negotiations and involve mortgage refinancing and other fun real estate procedures.

Income-Producing Assets

To state what may seem obvious: As a general rule, the greater the value of the marital assets before a divorce, the more complex the issues surrounding property division are going to be. If some of those assets themselves—like businesses or professional practices—produce income (more assets), it can get even trickier.

The added layer of complexity arises, in part, from the intertwining of the business with the personal and professional lives of either or both spouses, making it difficult to establish a clear valuation.

Basically, there are two primary challenges: First, there's the task of ascertaining the actual value of the business or practice itself. This involves assessing tangible assets like equipment, computers, and real estate as well as intangible assets such as a little something called goodwill.

The latter can be a particularly tough nut to crack because there are three types of goodwill: You've got *enterprise goodwill,* which is basically brand recognition. This can range all the way from the branding of the biggest corporate entities, like Walmart or Amazon (unless you're a Bezos or a Walton, this isn't you), to the usually hard-earned brand recognition within your local community. That one's more relatable.

Then you've got *personal (or pure) goodwill*, which is associated with an individual's expertise, knowledge, or standing in the community. For instance, a lawyer who has excelled in a specific field of law or a doctor specializing in a particular type of surgery would fall into this category. In these scenarios, the value of the professional practice is closely tied to the individual's distinct skills and reputation—remove that person, and you remove a significant portion of the value of that business.

There's also *transferable goodwill*. As the name suggests, this type of goodwill doesn't necessarily require a specific individual but can be transferred through training or coaching.

In addition to ascertaining the value of the business, you've got to figure out how much it actually earns. Many small businesses tend to blur the lines between personal and business expenses. I've often seen family members drawing a salary without contributing substantially to the business, and I've seen personal expenses written off as business-related costs. This stuff happens all the time and—while it may fly under the radar of the IRS—it's not going to fly when it comes to property division in a divorce case.

If all of this sounds like it might get pretty pricey, there's a reason for that: It's pretty pricey!

In cases when divorcing parties can't agree on the value of a business (factoring in the actual earnings, which often requires an accountant), the responsibility falls to the judge to determine the value based on the evidence presented by the parties. Ideally, the parties can agree on the value of the business during the divorce proceedings. If they can't, however, there are a series of processes they'll have to follow to figure it out.

The typical course of action involves each party hiring their own business appraiser. These appraisers independently assess the business and provide valuation opinions. Then the parties present their respective appraisals, each arguing to the court why theirs is more accurate.

Sometimes the parties agree to streamline the process by hiring a single appraiser. Ideally, both sides will agree to what that appraiser comes up with. Of course, it doesn't always work out ideally, and disputes arise. So, a second opinion is needed, which takes us back to the previous step.

This valuation process typically spans three to four months and can cost between $10,000 and $50,000. Maybe it'll cost less; maybe it'll cost more. It all depends on the size and complexity of the business being evaluated.

Divorce and Retirement Plans

If you and your spouse have retirement plans that started during (or, with long-term marriages, even before) the marriage, they're considered a marital asset. They're going to get divvied up. The primary tool for dividing most types of retirement plans is a qualified domestic relations order. This QDRO, as it's known, allows for the lawful division of assets between spouses, ensuring that the non-owning spouse can receive a portion of the retirement benefits.

There are literally tons of books about retirement plans, so I'm not going to dive too deep into the different varieties; rather, I'll give you a brief overview of how some of the more common types are divided in divorce.

Most employer-sponsored plans—like 401(k)s and 403(b)s—fall into the category of defined contribution plans: You pay in a certain amount each paycheck (often your employer will pay in a certain amount too), and the plan provider invests that money. A portion of the dividends of that investment gets added to the value of your plan.

Dividing a defined contribution plan typically involves determining the portion of the account that accrued during the marriage. This often includes contributions made and any investment gains during the marriage.

Defined benefit plans—good, old-fashioned pensions—provide a fixed benefit based on factors like salary and years of service. They promise a specific payout upon retirement, and QDROs play a crucial role in spec-ifying how the benefits will be divided (usually as either a percentage or a specific amount).

Individual retirement accounts, or IRAs, are often held individually and are distinct from employer-sponsored plans. They may include contributions from both spouses and don't necessarily require a QDRO. Instead, a divorce decree or settlement agreement can outline the division of IRA assets.

Regardless of which type of retirement plan you have, you're not going to want to DIY. The tax implica-tions can be too great, and there can be other penalties for withdrawing too much too soon. Not only that, but many of these plans also have required minimum distributions (RMDs), meaning you get penalized for *not* taking money. These can play a role in property division as well.

Property Division and Taxes
Speaking of tax implications, as with so many aspects of our American lives, Uncle Sam will want in on the action of your divorce. Here are some key considerations.

- **Transfer of assets:** When assets are transferred between spouses as part of the divorce settlement, it's essential to understand the tax consequences. The good news is that transfers directly between spouses are generally not subject to capital gains or gift taxes, but that doesn't mean you're home free.

- **Capital gains taxes:** Selling assets like real estate or investments (as opposed to transferring them) may trigger a capital gains tax. Special considerations may apply to the marital home, and the timing of the sale can impact the tax liability.

- **Maintenance and tax deductions:** Alimony payments made by one spouse to the other are not tax-deductible for the payer. However, tax laws have undergone changes (and change all the time), so it's important to be aware of the current rules.

- **Dependency exemptions and child tax credits:** Rules about who is exempt from taxes because of dependents and who is eligible for child-related tax credits can affect the amount each parent owes. Determining who gets to claim these benefits should be done in the divorce settlement.

- **Property sales and losses:** In some cases, selling marital property at a loss may have limited tax benefits. Understanding the rules surrounding capital losses and how they can be used is important when planning property sales.

- **Timing of divorce:** The timing of the divorce during the tax year can affect the filing status of the parties. Whether you file as married, single, or head of household can impact tax brackets, deductions, and credits.

As I stated earlier, there's a direct link between the amount of "stuff" you and your spouse have accumulated during your marriage and the complexity of the property division issues when you divorce. The costs of your breakup will likely increase right along with that complexity as you add appraisers, accountants, and real estate and tax attorneys to your payroll.

While there are certain guidelines courts have to follow when it comes to property division, there can be—as with so many aspects of divorce law—wide areas of latitude and discretion, not just within jurisdictions but with individual judges.

You really don't want to go it alone. With a good, qualified, and experienced divorce attorney, you won't have to.

CHAPTER 9
Let's Make a Divorce Deal—It's All About Negotiation

HOW TO NEGOTIATE THE BEST RESULT IN A DIVORCE CASE

Many people, when contemplating divorce, envision stressful hours in a courtroom, their attorney facing off against their spouse's attorney in front of a judge. In reality, this hardly ever happens.

The vast majority of divorce cases are settled through some form of negotiation. This doesn't mean that everything I've told you thus far, based on my own extensive experience, about how judges may look at different specific issues doesn't apply; it absolutely does. In most cases, however, these judicial viewpoints and considerations are applied to a divorce agreement already hammered out behind the scenes between you, your soon-to-be ex, and your respective attorneys. It's the judge's job to make sure this agreement adheres to the laws and standards of your state or jurisdiction—yet another reason to have a good attorney.

There are cases when the involved parties don't even meet the judge. When it comes to mitigating the emotional and financial costs of divorce as much as possible, this is actually the best-case scenario. (Hence the need to "keep it civil.")

In this chapter, we'll look at how to effectively prepare for negotiating, the different forms these negotiations can take, and the sequence in which specific issues are generally negotiated.

Prep Work

As I mentioned in chapter 5, the more information you can provide your lawyer before negotiations begin—the more "legwork" you can help your attorney avoid—the more efficiently they'll be able to handle your case. And, in many cases, the less it's going to cost you.

Here are some tips for making sure your lawyer has what they need. Some of these echo what I've already told you but are worth repeating.

- **Gather financial documents:** Collect all relevant financial documents, including bank statements, tax returns, investment portfolios, and property ownership records. A clear picture of the financial situation is essential for equitable distribution during divorce negotiations.

- **Create a detailed asset list:** Make a comprehensive list of all marital assets, including real estate, vehicles, valuables, and debts. This will help your attorney understand the extent of the marital estate and advocate for a fair division.

- **Establish a budget:** Prepare a realistic budget outlining your current and anticipated future expenses. This information can be used to support your financial needs and lifestyle during negotiations.

- **Document child custody preferences:** If children are involved, be prepared to articulate your preferred child custody arrangements. Maintain a record of your involvement in the

child's life, including daily routines, school
activities, and healthcare responsibilities.

- **Maintain good communication with
your attorney:** Establish open and honest
communication with your attorney, providing
them with all relevant information and
promptly responding to their requests.
This collaboration is crucial for building a
strong case.

- **Understand your legal rights:** Educate
yourself about divorce laws in your jurisdiction.
Knowing your rights and responsibilities will
empower you during negotiations and help you
make informed decisions.

 FOUR ROADS TO CONCLUDING
A DIVORCE

Four Roads to Resolution

There are basically four routes you can take to getting
your divorce case resolved. In ascending order of their
complexity (and their usual cost), they are negotiation,
mediation, arbitration, and litigation.

Negotiation

Negotiation is usually the starting point of a divorce agreement. You and your lawyer will negotiate the various issues with your spouse and their lawyer. This is typically an ongoing process, etched out over weeks or months through meetings, phone calls, and emails. It allows for open communication, enabling both parties to express their preferences, concerns, and priorities.

Negotiation offers flexibility—decisions made by the parties themselves empower them to tailor agreements to their unique circumstances. Your attorney, of course, will play a vital role in this process, providing legal advice, advocating for your interests, and assisting in crafting mutually acceptable solutions. The focus is on reaching a fair and comprehensive settlement that both parties find agreeable.

Mediation

If negotiations break down, your judge will usually order mediation, in which a neutral third party facilitates the negotiation process. This mediator is usually an attorney or retired judge (our firm often plays this role) who assists the spouses in communicating effectively, guiding them toward common ground and exploring potential solutions. Unlike a judge, the mediator does not make decisions but encourages collaborative problem-solving.

Mediation works particularly well when a less adversarial approach is desired, as it promotes cooperation and empowers the parties to actively participate in shaping the final agreement.

Mediation involves all the parties actually sitting in a room together, so if you and your spouse can't stand the sight of one another, it may not be feasible. Naturally, mediators cost more money; their fee is usually divided equally among the parties, although the payment for the mediator can sometimes be its own negotiation.

Arbitration

Arbitration is an alternative dispute resolution in which a neutral third party, known as the arbitrator, is appointed to act as a private judge. In arbitration, spouses present their cases—including evidence and arguments, just like in a courtroom trial—and the arbitrator renders decisions on contested issues. The primary distinction lies in the arbitrator's authority, which can be either binding or nonbinding (in essence, either a court can enforce it or not).

In my experience, arbitration is pretty rare, but it does happen. It can be more expensive than mediation, but if it's binding, it can be used to bypass the courts altogether.

Litigation

This is the one most folks considering divorce think about (and have nightmares about). It's the worst-case scenario, the last resort, the situation that negotiation, mediation, or perhaps arbitration aims to avoid.

You *really* don't want to go here. A good, experienced divorce attorney won't want to go here, either. In fact, you should add "anxious to take your divorce case to trial" to those red flags I mentioned in chapter 3. Here are some of the reasons you want to avoid litigation like the plague:

- **More stress, more money:** As you're learning, divorce can be emotionally draining and financially costly under the best of circumstances. Litigation is both, but on steroids—it can increase the money you'll spend and the stress you'll have to endure almost exponentially.

- **Less control:** In negotiations and mediations, you're in the driver's seat, even if it seems like you and your spouse are in different vehicles going different directions. But in a courtroom setting, decisions regarding the divorce settlement and issues such as property division, spousal support, and child custody are ultimately in the hands of the judge, and you're just a passenger on their bus.

- **A lot more time:** Time is money; time is stress. Litigation often involves lengthy court procedures, including discovery, motions, and trial dates, which can take months or even years to play out.

- **Airing your dirty laundry:** Courtroom proceedings are generally open to the public, meaning that personal and sensitive information may become part of the public record. Do you really want everyone to know your business?

- **Heightened hostility:** Litigation tends to foster an adversarial environment, pitting one spouse against the other in a win-lose scenario (even though, as I said earlier, there really are no winners in divorce). This heightened hostility can further strain relationships, especially when there are kids involved, and may hinder effective co-parenting in the post-divorce period.

- **Limited creativity in resolutions:** In litigation, judges apply established legal principles to make decisions that adhere to their jurisdiction's statutes and guidelines, which can limit flexibility and creativity in crafting solutions tailored to the unique needs and preferences of the parties. It's important to keep in mind that—of all the parties involved in your divorce case—the judge will probably know the least about the nuances of individual issues.

SEQUENCE OF NEGOTIATING A
DIVORCE SETTLEMENT

Sequence of Negotiations

Again, the overwhelming majority of divorce cases aren't going to come to litigation. So let's talk about the main issues in most proceedings and the order in which they're usually taken on.

Given the sensitive nature of child custody decisions, the weight given to the child's best interests, and the impact the arrangements can have on subsequent issues, these are often the initial focus in divorce proceedings with kids involved. You and your spouse will negotiate a parenting plan detailing who has legal custody and how often and for how long the noncustodial parent gets to see the kids (more on this in chapter 6). The amount of child support the noncustodial parent must pay is based on the resulting arrangement (covered in chapter 7).

Once the child custody issues have been resolved, you'll tackle property division. As detailed in chapter 8, you'll negotiate and collaborate on fair distributions of assets and debts.

As negotiations of child custody/support and property division often directly impact any sort of spousal support or alimony arrangement, this is usually the last arrangement to be addressed, and it's covered in chapter 7 as well.

I simply cannot emphasize enough (which is why I keep harping on it) that a "successful" divorce isn't about winning or losing, because it's always a costly, painful, stressful, lose-lose situation. Rather, success is determined by the degree to which this chapter of your life can come to a close with the least cost, the least pain, and the least stress.

In a divorce, negotiation is as close to win-win as you're going to get.

CHAPTER 10
Turning the Page—
Life after Divorce

NEW RELATIONSHIPS POST-DIVORCE

Divorce is a sad, stressful, life-changing chapter in anyone's story, an unexpected twist on what you once felt in your heart was meant to last "till death do us part." Happily ever after.

But what comes *after* happily ever after?

This last chapter of my book is all about writing the next chapter of yours. I offer these words not as a longtime divorce attorney but as a human being who has witnessed the lives of countless others who have gone through exactly what you're going through now and come out on the other side.

A New Relationship with Your Ex

Navigating a post-divorce relationship with your ex requires a delicate balance of communication and boundaries. Start by acknowledging the end of the romantic connection and accepting that the dynamics will markedly shift. You're no longer lovers; you may not even be friends. Yet there's a good chance—especially if you have children—that your former partner in life will remain a part of your life for many years to come.

Establishing clear boundaries is crucial to preventing misunderstandings and ensuring a respectful coexistence. It may involve setting guidelines for communication, defining roles in shared responsibilities, and clarifying expectations.

Effective communication—the lack of which may well have contributed to the marriage ending in the first place—becomes a cornerstone in this new phase. Maintaining an open and honest dialogue will allow you to focus on practical matters and avoid unnecessary emotional entanglements.

Try to cultivate a sense of empathy and understanding of your ex-spouse's perspective. It may seem impossible—you and your ex may have come to view each other as evil incarnate. But just as maintaining at least a modicum of civility is necessary during your divorce proceedings, so too is it needed for a healthier post-divorce relationship.

Ultimately, the goal is to transform the connection from a romantic partnership into a cooperative and supportive alliance for the benefit of all involved.

A New Relationship with Your Kids

If you have children, you know that their world has been turned upside-down. Often they blame themselves; other times, they may blame you and/or your ex. Or it could be a combination of all of these. Either way, they need your unconditional love and support more than ever.

The tragedy of divorce can provide an opportunity to "start fresh" with your kids, to remedy any mistakes you made as a parent when you took their constant presence for granted, to strengthen bonds that may have weakened. Presenting a united front with your ex on all matters pertaining to the kids, showing them that your love transcends the strife, is a good start. Being more present in their lives, attending school events and extracurricular activities, is another way to rebuild and strengthen those bonds. So is encouraging an environment where your kids feel comfortable expressing their emotions and concerns.

If all of this seems somehow familiar, it's because I talked about these things in chapter 6. The steps you take to ensure that you get the best outcome in your child custody arrangements are the same steps that can help ensure a strong, lasting relationship with your children in the future.

A New Financial Reality

Divorce often brings a significant shift in financial circumstances. In fact, there are very few instances in which someone coming out of divorce is in better shape financially than when they went in. Where there were once two incomes in a single household, there's now a single income in two. Whatever assets you and your ex accumulated during the marriage have been divided. If you have children and are the noncustodial spouse, you have child support payments. There may be maintenance on top of that.

Understanding and adapting to this new reality is a crucial aspect of moving forward. Take stock of your financial situation, including assets, debts, and ongoing expenses. If necessary, consult with a financial advisor to create a realistic budget and financial plan.

Be proactive; be realistic. Don't make a bad situation worse.

Physical and Emotional Self-Care

As you already well know, divorce can take a toll on your physical and emotional well-being. This doesn't all magically disappear just because the judge signed your decree.

Just as taking care of your body and mind is crucial during your divorce, so too is it after the dust has settled. Maintain a routine that prioritizes your health, including regular exercise, a balanced diet, and sufficient sleep. Continue to acknowledge and process your feelings; don't be afraid to seek support from friends, family, or professional therapists who can offer guidance. Allow yourself the space to grieve the end of the relationship while focusing on personal growth and resilience. Consider activities that bring joy and fulfillment—rediscover passions and hobbies that may have taken a back seat during the marriage.

Taking care of yourself isn't selfish; it's a necessary step toward healing and building a strong foundation for the next chapter of your life.

The road to divorce is paved with heartbreak, stress, and uncertainty, a disappointing departure from the storybook ending you had envisioned. I truly hope that I've been able to make that road a bit smoother and to help you better understand what the journey will entail.

ABOUT THE AUTHOR

Attorney Jeff Hughes is the CEO and co-founder of Sterling Lawyers, one of the largest and most influential family law firms in the United States.

As the oldest of eight siblings, Jeff began his legal journey from humble beginnings. He grew up in a broken home that seemed to always hover slightly above the poverty line. He bounced around, living in fifteen homes before the age of eighteen.

He worked his way through college, holding up to three jobs at a time. Jeff did not have the grades or credentials to attend a prestigious law school, so he chose the one with the lowest tuition that would accept him.

After law school, Jeff received two job offers: One was with the state's attorney in his hometown of Edwardsville, Illinois. The other was with a small community law firm in Menomonee Falls, Wisconsin.

He chose the law firm job for the simple reason that it seemed to offer him a solid path out of poverty and into financial stability. This turned out to be a life-defining decision because it introduced him to family law. The rest is history, as Jeff quickly realized that his "super talent" lay in connecting with and serving family clients.

Today, Jeff is a devoted follower of Jesus. He and his wife, Winona, live in Wisconsin with all six of their children nearby. He cherishes his responsibilities as a husband and dad. When he's not doing that, you'll find him at the CrossFit gym, playing his guitar, straining muscles on the pickleball court, casting for fish, or thinking about eating warm chocolate chip cookies.

www.ingramcontent.com/pod-product-compliance
Lightning Source LLC
Chambersburg PA
CBHW021458180326
41458CB00051B/6873/J